What Happens When Young Women Say Yes to God

LYSA TERKEURST AND HOPE TERKEURST HOUSER

HARVEST HOUSE PUBLISHERS
EUGENE, OREGON

Unless otherwise indicated, all Scripture verses are taken from the Holy Bible, New International Version®· NIV®. Copyright © 1973, 1978, 1984, 2011, by Biblica, Inc.® Used by permission of Zondervan. All rights reserved worldwide. (www.zondervan.com)

Verses marked MSG are taken from The Message. Copyright © by Eugene H. Peterson 1993, 1994, 1995, 1996, 2000, 2001, 2002. Used by permission of NavPress Publishing Group.

Verses marked NASB are taken from the New American Standard Bible®, © 1960, 1962, 1963, 1968, 1971, 1972, 1973, 1975, 1977, 1995 by The Lockman Foundation. Used by permission. (www .Lockman.org)

Cover by Connie Gabbert Design + Illustration

Cover photo © Bogdan Sonjachnyj / Shutterstock

Backcover author photos by Sean Lyon and Amy Riley Photography

Published in association with the literary agency of Fedd & Company, Inc., PO Box 341973, Austin, TX 78734.

"Yes in Action" pieces contributed by Hope TerKeurst Houser.

WHAT HAPPENS WHEN YOUNG WOMEN SAY YES TO GOD

Copyright © 2013 by Lysa TerKeurst
Published by Harvest House Publishers
Eugene, Oregon 97408
www.harvesthousepublishers.com

    ISBN 978-0-7369-7286-4 (pbk.)
    ISBN 978-0-7369-7287-1 (eBook)

The Library of Congress has catalogued the edition as follows:

Library of Congress Cataloging-in-Publication Data

    TerKeurst, Lysa.
    What happens when young women say yes to God / Lysa TerKeurst and Hope TerKeurst.
        p. cm
    Includes bibliographical references.
    ISBN 978-0-7369-5455-6 (pbk.)
    1. Christian women—Religious life. I. Title.
    BV4527.T4645 2013
    248.8'43—dc23

                          2012043873

Printed in the United States of America

18 19 20 21 22 23 24 25 26 / BP-JC / 10 9 8 7 6 5 4 3 2 1

Acknowledgments

Art TerKeurst—You are the love of my life. Thank you for modeling to our family what it looks like to say yes to God.

Hope TerKeurst—What a joy it is to be the mom of such a beautiful young woman who says yes to God. I'm blessed to call you my daughter, and I cannot wait to see what God has in store for you. Thank you for helping make this book what it is.

Ashley, Brooke, Jackson, and Mark—I love you and pray this message is the greatest lesson I've taught you as a mom. Keep saying yes to God…forever.

Hope Lyda—Thank you for your dedication to this project. You have an amazing heart and have invested countless hours in this project. God sees you and treasures you!

Esther Fedorkevich—I love calling you my agent, but even more you are a terrific friend. Thank you…for everything.

Leah Kimenhour—The way you've stepped into your role with wisdom beyond your years amazes me. And you sport a pretty killer sock bun too! Thank you for your hours of help with this project.

Lori Gardner, Lindsay Kreis, and Meredith Brock—Wow… there aren't enough words to tell you how thankful I am for all you do…and even more for how much you care.

The Proverbs 31 Team—My friends, my family. Thank you for being so dedicated in furthering the kingdom.

Contents

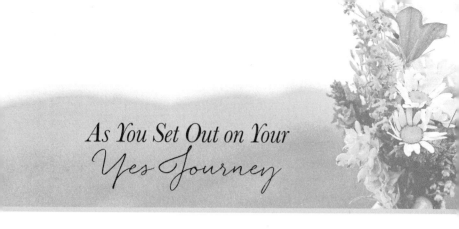

As You Set Out on Your *Yes Journey*

We are about to discover how God's love shapes our hearts and our individual paths of purpose. It's an amazing journey. We won't want to miss any of the messages He has for us. In this book you will discover the following features. Each is created to make the truths and wonders of faith more three-dimensional in your life.

Yes Factor

The gifts of the yes journey are plentiful. The Yes Factors highlight some of the most amazing treasures you'll discover along the way. They are ready to tweet so you can share with your friends, classmates, and online communities to encourage them.

You're Invited

Each chapter has a special invitation to say yes to God in a new way. Take time with these and pray about how you'll respond to the call to embrace God's best.

God's Word for You

God speaks to us through the Bible. Scripture is not a gathering of material meant for people ages ago. It was written *for you*. This feature includes questions for group or personal study, reflection points, and verse explorations to get God's Word from the page to your heart.

Living Y.E.S. (Your Extraordinary Story)

Only you can live your extraordinary story. No one else is designed by God to live this moment and all of your tomorrows. These insights and journal questions will help you understand the uniqueness, incredible value, and power of having a yes heart for God.

Yes in Action: A Note from Hope's Yes Journey

My teenage daughter Hope shares four personal accounts of listening to God and following His lead. My prayer is that these glimpses of another young woman facing the difficulties and delights of obedience will encourage you to put your yes into action daily.

My Yes Journey Notes

At the back of this book are several note pages so you have a convenient place to write down the ideas, challenges, special verses, prayer needs, and discoveries you experience while starting your yes journey.

Ready for Something Better

Most of us long for something better. Different. Special. *Extraordinary.*

We desire something more meaningful than day-to-day survival.

And the amazing thing is that even before we can name this desire, God has placed it within us and is drawing us closer to Him through that desire. Our hunger to be special and to do special things is our spiritual hunger to have an extraordinary relationship with God.

But how do we leave normal behind and head toward extraordinary?

We start a journey! It's the amazing, transforming, anything-but-normal journey you'll begin the day you say yes to God and to the amazing faith life He has planned for you.

Let's begin at the starting place—right here, right now. Imagine with me that this is your day.

Beep. Beep. The notification of a text message wakes you up before your alarm. It's a friend reminding you to bring money for the school fund-raiser and asking if you will make signs during lunch. As you sneak into the kitchen hoping to grab a bagel and glass of cranberry juice without being spoken to, your parents greet you with good-mornings and then insist you walk the dog before school.

You get to school with only a second to wave to friends. You settle into the assigned seat of the first class and do a mental happy dance because you finished your project early. The celebration is squelched because the teacher asks you to help a student who doesn't understand yesterday's assignment.

During lunch you finally get a chance to catch up with your best friend, but she still wants to talk through every event leading to her breakup with her boyfriend—five months ago. You listen for a while and pat her on the back for consolation, but you're thinking, *At least you had a boyfriend. My parents won't even let me date.*

The list goes on, right? A regular, ordinary day includes a lot of requests from a lot of people in your life. There are expectations. And even when you know the right thing to do, you don't have much joy when you follow through. *What's the point?* you think. *It's all so ordinary and leading nowhere.*

Even if people want good things from you and of you, it's tempting to say no. Nope. Uh-uh. No, thank you. I helped yesterday. Ask so-and-so. The dog ate my homework and my backpack and my computer.

There are lots of ways to say no.

When God asks you to do something, it can spark the desire to act as if you didn't hear Him. It's tempting to rattle off your memorized top five excuses for getting out of something that might be challenging, humbling, or out of your comfort zone.

In fact, sometimes God asks us to do things that seem a bit crazy at the time. We can't see the big picture the way He does. We can't imagine how our one yes during an ordinary day can become something extraordinary when He uses it for His purposes.

But, you see, this is where we get confused. When we say yes to God, our days are no longer ordinary or normal. In fact, there is no such thing as a typical day. Once you make the leap of faith to say yes to God, you will discover the power that answer holds in your relationship with Him, others, and yourself. There's *nothing* ordinary about what's ahead for you. Are you nervous? Are you looking around you and thinking, *Maybe normal is okay? What is God going to ask of me when I say yes?*

Believe me, I understand this as well as anyone. I can be stubborn. I can be resistant to being told what to do. And I've had plenty of times when I wanted to do *anything* but what God was asking me to do. In fact, I was someone who never left home without having my top five excuses list handy. This *was* me...that is, until God opened my eyes to the incredible, blow-my-socks-off power of saying yes to Him.

It all started the day He told me to give away my Bible.

My ministry as a writer and a speaker gives me the chance to visit churches, women's groups, and conferences. On this particular day, I was heading home after a long schedule of speaking and I was wiped out. All I wanted was to get to my assigned seat on the plane and settle in for a nap. Imagine my absolute delight at being the only person seated in my row. I was just about to close my eyes when two last-minute passengers made their way to my row and took their seats.

Reluctantly, I decided to skip my nap. The last thing I wanted was to fall asleep and snore, drool, or, worse yet, wake up with my head resting on the guy's shoulder beside me. I did not need another most embarrassing moment, so I pulled a manuscript out of my bag and started reading.

"What are you working on?" the guy asked. I told him I was a Christian writer. He smiled and said he thought God was a very interesting topic. I agreed and asked him a few questions about his beliefs. Before long I found myself reaching into my bag and pulling out my Bible, walking him through some key verses that dealt with the issues he was facing. He kept asking questions, and I kept praying God would give me answers.

All of a sudden I felt God tugging at my heart to give this man my Bible. Now, this was not just any Bible. This was my everyday, highlighted, underlined, written in, and tearstained Bible. I hesitated, but God's message was clear. I was to give away my Bible.

I pulled out old church bulletins and other papers I had tucked inside the covers, took a deep breath, sighed, and placed it in the man's hands. "I'd like for you to have my Bible," I said.

Astonished, he started to hand it back to me, saying he couldn't possibly accept such a gift. "God told me to give it to you," I insisted. "Sometimes the God of the universe pauses in the midst of all His creation to touch the heart of one person. Today, He paused for you."

The man took my Bible and made two promises. First, he said he would read it, and, second, someday he would pass it on, doing for someone else what I'd done for him.

Before I knew it, the plane landed and we were saying our goodbyes. As I stepped into the aisle preparing to disembark, the women on the other side of the businessman reached out and grabbed my arm. She'd been staring out the window the entire time we were flying, and I thought she'd been ignoring us. But her tearstained face told a different story. In a tone so hushed I could barely hear her, she whispered, "Thank you. What you shared today has changed my life." I put my hand on hers and whispered back, "You're welcome." Then a knot caught in my throat as tears welled up in my eyes. I didn't have another Bible to give away, so I gave her one of my books and hugged her goodbye. It has been said that we are to tell the whole world about Jesus, using words only if necessary. I saw this powerful truth come to life. Though I never spoke to this lady about Jesus, she saw Him through my obedience. How humbling. How profound.

As I got off the plane that day, I could barely hold back my tears. Three people's hearts were radically changed. I believe the businessman came to know Jesus as his Lord and Savior. I believe the same is true for the lady. But my heart was changed in a dramatic way as well. I was overjoyed at what God had done, but I was

Yes Factor

Open your heart to God's love. Open your life to His calling. Open your mouth to praise Him.

also brokenhearted by the flood of thoughts that came to mind recounting times I'd told God no. How tragic to miss His divine appointments.

I kept wondering, *How many times have I told You no, God? How many times have I walked right past an extraordinary moment You had shaped for me because I was too tired, too insecure, too caught up in drama, or too selfish? How often do I miss out on experiencing You?* I lifted up my heart to the Lord and whispered, "Please forgive me for all those noes. Right now I say yes, Lord. I say yes to You before I even know what You might ask me to do. I simply want You to see a yes-heart in me."

Several minutes after exiting the plane, I was heading toward my connecting gate when I spotted the businessman again. He stopped me to tell me he'd been praying and thanking God for what happened on the plane. We swapped business cards, and, though we lived several states apart, I knew we'd stay in touch.

About a month later he called to tell me his life had totally changed. He'd taken a week off from work to read the Bible, and he'd already shared his testimony with numerous people. God was definitely pursuing this man in a serious way! When I asked him what his favorite verse was, he said it was Proverbs 3:5-6: "Trust in the LORD with all your heart and lean not on your own understanding; in all your ways submit to him, and he will make your paths straight." I thought to myself, *Wow! Look at how God has already answered that for my new friend.*

He also told me that after reading the Bible he knew he needed to get involved in a church, so he'd decided to visit a large church in his town. On his way there he passed another church, and a strong feeling came over him to turn his car around and go back. So he did. When he got to his seat in the sanctuary, he opened up his bulletin and gasped. Inside the bulletin he saw an announcement that I was to be the speaker at an upcoming women's conference. He said he felt as though, once again, God was confirming His active presence.

That day on the plane, when God impressed on my heart to give this man my Bible, I did not know what would happen. This man might have thrown my Bible into the nearest airport trash can for all I knew. Normally, I would've come up with a hundred reasons *not* to give my Bible away, but that day something changed in me. That day, for the first time, I truly heard the call of a woman who says yes to God: "Live your extraordinary story of faith."

This journey we are taking together is life changing.

1

An Extraordinary Life Awaits

The amazing adventure of living your life and faith in extraordinary ways is up ahead. Here is the most wonderful truth: God designed it for *you*. And this journey cannot be lived out by anyone else. God made you as a special, nobody-else-like-you young woman, and He has a plan for your life. Do you feel it? Do you believe it? When you get up in the morning, do you think about how your day can only be lived out by the incredible you? Your family knows you and your quirky habits, and your friends share common interests, but nobody else is taking your steps through your day.

The extraordinary faith journey begins the moment you say yes to God and yes to the story He is creating through your heart, abilities, dreams, and faithfulness. It's not just a special story—it's an extraordinary one you and God experience together.

When we feel a tug on our heart and a stirring in our soul for more, we are often afraid to venture past our comfort zone. Outside our comfort zone, however, is where we experience the true awesomeness of God. But you have to take the plunge. How ready are you?

Notice that I didn't ask "How perfect are you?" Perfection is highly overrated. I think at this point it is important for me to paint an accurate picture of what my life looks like before you imagine me as this super calm, amazingly organized and disciplined person who spends hours on her knees in prayer. Truth? My to-do list rarely gets accomplished. My emotions have been known to run wild, and my patience can run thin. I get pushed to the limit by everyday aggravations, such as a summer's worth of pictures getting erased from my digital camera. Or a dog who runs away at the most inconvenient times. And I've had times when I step outside my comfort zone and fear causes me to second-guess myself and God's plan.

Can you relate? Great! No matter what your life is like, you're a young woman made to say yes to God. Even if you're juggling all the craziness life can throw your way, when you simply whisper yes, you are equipped to start your extraordinary story of following God. "Yes, Lord. I want Your patience to override my desire to fly off the handle." "Yes, Lord. I want Your strength to keep my emotions in check when my family and friends drive me nuts." "Yes, Lord. I want Your courage to accept challenges that intimidate me." "Yes, Lord. I want to see my great value as Your daughter so I don't worry about what other people think."

You don't need perfect circumstances to say yes to God. You don't need the perfect religious attitude or all the answers to religious questions. You simply have to give to God all of the thoughts, worries, people, drama, and struggles that occupy your attention and your heart. You simply have to speak the answer God is longing to hear spill from your lips. "Yes, God."

The Daily Yes Prayer

Each day when I wake up, I pray a very simple prayer before my feet even hit the floor. I encourage you to write your own or use this prayer so you can experience your extraordinary God in extraordinary ways.

God, I want to see You.
God, I want to hear You.
God, I want to know You.
God, I want to follow hard after You.
And even before I know what I will face today, I say yes to You.

This simple act of surrender each morning will prepare your eyes to see Him, your ears to hear Him, your mind to perceive Him, and your heart to receive Him. This is how to live expecting to experience God.

You see, we have become so familiar with God and yet still so unaware of Him. We turn the mysterious into something ordinary, even boring. We construct careful reasons for our rules and sensible whys for our behavior. All the while our soul is longing for a richer experience—one that allows us to escape the limits of sight, sound, touch, taste, and smell and journey to a place of wild, wonder, and passion.

Young women who say yes to God will see life like few others.

And you will be drawn in and embraced by a love like no other. You don't have to wait until the next time you're in church to experience God because you can sense God's presence all around you, all through your day. Instead of going through the motions of life, you'll pursue the adventure of the moment-by-moment divine story and lessons God is unfolding.

When you say yes, you can *expect* to see God, to hear from Him, and to be absolutely filled by His peace and joy.

The Holy and the Ordinary

Embracing a holy God in the middle of life's everyday activities will change your life. God's surprises of good and wondrous experiences will take your breath away, but you might not always feel happy about the changes. I can't let you think that being a young woman who says yes to God means everything is always easy. There will be times when you experience the sting of heartache, frustration, uncertainty, failure, and loss, but now there will be new ways of dealing with those hard times. A holy way.

I had one of those experiences recently. I simply wanted to throw my hands in the air, throw my computer out the window, and cry out to God, "You have hurt my feelings, and I'm just a little unnerved and upset!"

I was at a friend's lake house to devote three days to a writing project. After the first night of working hard, I had gone to bed excited about all I'd accomplished. I awakened the next morning ready to have the same kind of success. But as I opened up my document folder with great anticipation, I saw…nothing. Nothing! The project was nowhere to be found.

Refusing to panic, I asked for my friends' help. After two hours of searching, one of my friends gently looked at me and verbalized the truth we'd all come to know. "It's gone, Lysa. You are going to have to start over."

What!

Wait a minute, I thought. *I have said yes to God today and had a great quiet time. I just know He can and will help me find this.* But for whatever reason, my document was gone and God had chosen not to bring it back. Tears filled my eyes as bitterness started to creep in my heart. Why would He allow this? My friend could sense my despair and gently replied, "Lysa, recently when something like this happened to me, someone told me to look at my loss as a sacrifice of praise to God. It is so hard in today's abundance to give God a true sacrifice, but losing two thousand words and a whole day's work would qualify. Give this to Him without feeling bitter."

I resisted slapping my well-meaning friend as she then broke into singing praise songs. By the second stanza, I actually found myself joining in with a lighter heart and a resilient spirit.

Have you ever lost something that had required great effort and care on your part? Sometimes it isn't a school project or a writing assignment we've invested in; rather, it's a relationship. If you've ever said goodbye to a friend because of a move or because you find yourself taking a different path, you've experienced what felt like an unfair loss of time, effort, and heart. The loss of "what could've been" can be very disappointing. When you care about anything, it makes you more vulnerable. The risk is higher

Yes Factor

Saying yes to God isn't about perfect performance, but rather perfect surrender to Him.

because more of your heart and soul is vested in the outcome. This is exactly why these times can be lifted up as a praise offering.

Being a young woman who says yes to God is about trusting Him even when you can't understand why He requires some of the things He does. It also means that once you've said yes to God, you refuse to turn back, even when things get hard.

This kind of obedience invites you to embrace a bigger vision for your life. When you look at your everyday circumstances with God's perspective, everything changes. You realize that He uses each circumstance, each person who crosses your path, and each encounter you have with Him as a divine appointment. Each day counts, and every action and reaction matters. God absolutely loves to take ordinary people and do extraordinary things in them, through them, and with them.

It's a Party

Imagine that you've planned a wonderful surprise party for your best friend. The guests have all arrived. You've loaded the decorated dining room table with her favorite junk food and healthy preferences. Everything is ready for the guest of honor. You can barely wait for the big moment of "Surprise!" because you know your friend will feel so loved and celebrated.

Finally, the time has come. And gone. Your friend is late. Your other friends are whispering in the darkened living room and trying unsuccessfully to hold back waves of laughter. Suddenly, your cell phone rings. Your friend's image appears on the screen. "Shhh!" you say to the others just before answering the call.

"Hey, where are you?" you ask casually.

Instead of saying she's on her way, your friend says she's too tired to come over and has decided to watch the last two episodes of her favorite show online. She's already in her pajamas and will check out whatever you wanted to show her tomorrow. You try to convince her that tonight is so much better and you really want to share something with her. But with a friendly "See you tomorrow, I promise," she hangs up.

But by tomorrow the guests will be gone, the leftover food will be stored away, and the party that never started will be over.

How sad for the guest of honor, who missed her own surprise party! And how disappointing for you, the party planner who orchestrated the event with the hope of showing a friend how much she is loved.

God must feel the same way when we miss the "surprise parties" that await us each day. These are the divine appointments sprinkled throughout our day for us to experience when we pay attention to God's leading. He must be so disappointed when we don't hear or don't listen to Him redirecting us to hang up the phone and show up at the event He has planned with great care. It must break His heart when we brush aside something that not only would make us feel special and noticed by God, but also would allow us to join Him in making life a little sweeter for others.

Which Invitation Will You Accept?

How many times have you missed your own surprise party?

God reveals Himself and His activity to all of us, but it takes a desire for the extraordinary to embrace these encounters because they can cause extreme changes in our plans, our perspectives, and our passions. I don't know about you, but I'm not a huge fan of change.

Yet, when we protect ourselves from change, we're saying no to God and yes to a life that leaves us unmotivated and directionless. Let's pause for a second and give that another look. You *are* accepting an invitation at any given moment, but are you saying yes to whims, desires, and random paths? Or are you accepting God's invitation to your purposed, powerful faith story?

I can think of several times when I let fear override my faith. I said yes to my insecurities and worries instead of God's strength and certainty. Has this happened to you? Maybe you felt God leading you to say yes to Him, yet you didn't go out for a play, you held back from introducing yourself to a new girl at school, or you resisted telling a guy you like about your faith. Every day has chances like these to step forward in God's leading, but we have to be prepared and ready to notice these opportunities from Him. When we are prepared and we do step out in faith, He will bless our yes!

You're Invited...

to Attend God's Surprise Party for You

WHAT:

The party you don't want to miss! This is a gathering of God's best for you...love, grace, hope, promises, and the joy of His wonder and will. All the great surprises of faith.

WHEN:

This moment. Forget the excuses. Get ready for something extraordinary.

WHERE:

On the other side of the door. Don't hesitate. Open the door. God and the incredible surprises of the yes journey are waiting for you.

WHAT TO BRING:

Everything is provided...so leave behind all that is ordinary. You'll want to be able to receive the extraordinary gifts God has chosen just for you.

How to Make *HI*Story

I love the word "history" because when we break it down we see that it means "His story." Your personal history might have times of pain or trouble. There might be moments of sadness or loneliness. And your past might be littered with some mistakes, but God is a God of transformation. He uses each and every part of your history and present to make an extraordinary new story.

As I've spoken to a lot of young women from around the country, I've been saddened to discover how many miss out on the most exciting part of being a Christian—experiencing God and experiencing their extraordinary story through Him. This is the great gift of being a Christian. The gift isn't about perfection or becoming the most popular person in school because you are blessed. The gift is being able to live out *your* extraordinary story with and through God's amazing love. It's incredible.

Those who say they want *more* in their Christian life are often looking outside of their personal relationship with God for the secret. They want their church, their pastor, or someone or something else to be the missing piece. These supports can make your faith stronger, but it is your one-on-one experience with God that changes everything.

You and I are on our way to recognizing and experiencing what that "more" can look like. It's a relationship with God that allows us to

- know His voice
- live in expectation of His activity
- embrace a life totally sold out for Him

I suspect you desire such closeness with God. This fulfillment of this desire is real and amazing. And this incredible adventure starts with the wild willingness to say yes.

In today's world, it is radical to obey God's commands, listen to the Holy Spirit's convictions, and walk in Jesus' character. And we'll experience the amazing blessings God has in store for us when we speak that big, freeing "Yes, Lord." This response to God's call, His requests, and His hope for us will lead to a great, unforgettable faith story.

Don't stumble over the fear you won't be perfect and you'll likely mess up. Saying yes to God isn't about perfect performance, but rather perfect surrender to the Lord day by day. It's about experiencing the full blessing of God by giving your full attention to God when He asks you to trust Him. It's having the overwhelming desire to walk in the center of His will at every moment. The life of yes happens when you hear God, feel His nudges, participate in His activity, and experience His blessings in ways few people ever do.

The God of the universe wants to use you in great ways. Are you ready?

There is only one requirement for this adventure. We have to set *our* rules and agendas aside—our dos and don'ts—and follow God's command. His one requirement is so simple and yet so profound: *Say yes to Me.* That's it. That is the entire Bible, Old Testament and New, hundreds of pages, thousands of verses, all wrapped up in those four words.

God's Word for You

Psalm 19:7-10 says,

> The revelation of GOD is whole and pulls our lives
> together. The signposts of GOD are clear and point out
> the right road. The life-maps of GOD are right, showing
> the way to joy. The directions of GOD are plain and easy
> on the eyes. GOD's reputation is twenty-four-carat gold,
> with a lifetime guarantee. The decisions of GOD are accu-
> rate down to the nth degree. God's Word is better than
> a diamond, better than a diamond set between emeralds.
> You'll like it better than strawberries in spring, better than
> red, ripe strawberries (MSG).

What does this passage tell you about God's nature?

Which of these promises are ones you really needed to hear right
now? Why?

Read Deuteronomy 6:5. What might loving God with your heart,
soul, and strength look like in your daily life?

Psalm 16:7-9 says,

> I will bless the LORD who guides me; even at night my heart instructs me. I know the LORD is always with me. I will not be shaken, for he is right beside me. No wonder my heart is glad, and I rejoice. My body rests in safety.

Describe how these verses ease your worries or concerns.

Living Y.E.S. (Your Extraordinary Story)

Have you ever felt God leading you to do something? How did you respond?

What holds you back from going deeper in your relationship with God? Time? Intimidation? Doubt about the Bible's relevance to life? Worry about what others will say? Fear that God will let you down like people have? Write down which of these or other barriers come between you and an extraordinary faith right now.

How might God's love counter these obstacles?

Why are you ready now to experience God's great surprises for you?

In this chapter we read, "Being a young woman who says yes to God is about trusting Him even when you can't understand why He requires some of the things He does. It also means that once you've said yes to God, you refuse to turn back, even when things get hard."

List two ways you want to trust God by saying yes to Him this week.

1.

2.

What title would you give your extraordinary story?

Yes Prayer

Your extraordinary story unfolds each time you listen to God and follow His leading. Here is a prayer to lead you to each of God's sweet surprises for you.

Dear God, I am putting away all my excuses so I can fully celebrate who You are and who I am in You. Thank You for adopting me as Your child and loving me unconditionally. I want to grow closer to You as I trust You more completely. I know You will ask me to grow and to move outside of my comfort zone, but with Your strength and help, I'm ready to experience my extraordinary story. I say yes to You with great joy. In Jesus' name, amen.

2

Is That You, God?

Every day, God speaks to us. Sometimes He invites us to draw close and listen as He reveals Himself, His character, and His direction. Other times He calls to us to participate in His purposes. Still other times He simply whispers to remind us of His amazing love for us.

It is incredibly amazing to know God speaks to me! But I've found that many believers are missing this vital element in their relationship with Him. As I've talked with people about my own journey of yes, they are quick to ask how they might hear from God too. Maybe you have some of these same questions:

- How do I know if God is speaking to me?
- How do I discern whether it is His voice speaking or just my own idea?
- What if I feel God is telling me to do something that doesn't seem to make sense?

Though there is no magic formula for being able to discern God's voice, we can *learn* to recognize it the way we recognize the voices of those close to us by knowing Him as we know our family members, our best friends, and others who become our trusted mentors. When we know Him in this way, we can tell if what we're feeling led to do is from Him or not.

I'll be honest. Though I hear from God all the time, I've never heard His voice audibly. When He speaks to me, it's a certain impression on my heart I've come to recognize as Him. I've also learned to ask five key questions to help me determine if what I'm hearing is from God or not:

1. Does what I'm hearing line up with Scripture?
2. Is it consistent with God's character?
3. Is it being confirmed through messages I'm hearing at church or studying in my quiet times?
4. Is it beyond me?
5. Would it please God?

Asking these questions helps me figure out the difference between my thoughts and God's impressions. It's as though we are given a special map to and through His plan for us. It's exciting because we know we're heading into the wonderful yes journey, but we need to be prepared for uncertain times, questions, and doubts. You and I will face twists, turns, and intersections, and we'll need to know which way to go. But it's comforting to know that God's directions are never wrong.

Does What I'm Hearing Line Up with Scripture?

God will not speak to us or tell us to do something that is contrary to His Word, but unless we know Scripture, we won't be able to discern whether what we are hearing is consistent with the Word. The apostle Paul wrote, "Do not conform to the pattern of this world, but be transformed by the renewing of your mind. Then you will be able to test and approve what God's will is—his good, pleasing and perfect will" (Romans 12:2). God's Word is the language the Holy Spirit uses to help us understand what God is speaking to our hearts.

We must get into God's Word and let God's Word get into us. This will transform our mind and prepare it for whatever He wants to tell us. Then, as Paul wrote, we will be able to test and approve not just God's good will, and not just His pleasing will, but His perfect will.

The good news is that you don't need a seminary degree to read your Bible. A good rule of thumb is "simply start and start simply." Read a passage of Scripture and ask yourself these questions:

- Who is this passage speaking to?
- What is it saying to me?
- What direction is this passage giving?
- How might I need to change my way of thinking or acting as a result of this verse?
- What are some other verses that relate to this topic, both in the Old Testament and New Testament?

These questions are just a starting place. I encourage you to get a journal and start recording the verses you study and some of your personal experiences with the things you are learning as you read God's Word. These moments are not just experiences with a book. These are encounters with God's Word for *you.*

Is What I'm Hearing Consistent with God's Character?

God's Word provides rich information about His character. Understanding the character of someone we have a relationship with is essential. Think about one of your good friends. What has drawn you to her over the years? Why can you trust her? I know my closest friends are those who have strong character. I don't mean strong as in they are always the center of attention. I mean strong as in trustworthy, faithful, honest, dependable, and kind. I know about their character because I've witnessed the way they have handled conflict, heartache, temptations, and challenges. I know that when they're faced with the decision of whether to be generous or selfish, they choose to be generous. I know that when they're tempted to lie or to blame someone else for their mistakes, they choose to own up to their choices. I know because I've watched them and I've experienced their character in action.

Have you ever been around someone who says one thing but does another? Isn't that the worst? Well, God will *not* say things that are inconsistent with who He is. And He will not guide you in ways that go against His Word. The apostle Paul writes, "Those who live according to the flesh have their minds set on what the flesh desires; but those who live in accordance with the Spirit have their minds set on what the Spirit desires" (Romans 8:5). What is it that God's Spirit desires? Answering this question helps us understand God's character.

We find great insight into God's character in Galatians 5:22-23: "The fruit of the Spirit is love, joy, peace, patience, kindness, goodness, faithfulness, gentleness and self-control." These characteristics in a person's life are the evidence of Christ at work.

> The fruit of the Spirit is the spontaneous work of the Holy Spirit in us. The Spirit produces these character traits that are found in the nature of Christ. They are by-products of Christ's control—we can't obtain them by trying to get them without his help. If we want the fruit of the Spirit to grow in us, we must join our lives to his. We must know him, love him, remember him, and imitate him.[1]

If the fruit of the Spirit is our imitation of Him, then it must be consistent with God's character. When you feel God speaking to you, ask yourself, *Is what I'm hearing consistent with God's love, joy, peace, etc.?*

In addition to the fruit of the Spirit, God's character is revealed in a loving relationship with us. As we experience God personally, we come to know new names for Him. When we've experienced His provision, we come to know Him as our Provider. When we've experienced His soothing presence, we come to know Him as our Comforter. When we've experienced His amazing love, we come to know Him as the Great Lover of our souls.

If what you're hearing is consistent with God's character, ask the next question.

Is What I'm Hearing Being Confirmed Through Other Messages?

When God is speaking to me about a particular issue, I cannot escape it. Around every corner is a sermon or Bible study lesson or speaker's topic or conversation with a friend consistent with what I've been hearing from God in my time alone with Him.

Do you spend time alone with God? We shouldn't wait to hear from Him just on Sunday mornings or during a weekly Bible study or when a speaker comes to town. These are places to confirm what we've heard in our time alone, where we are personally studying God's Word, learning more about His character, and listening for His voice. If Sunday morning is our only encounter with God and His Word, we miss out on this amazing chance to have His voice and message confirmed and reinforced at other times. And believe me, you and I don't want to miss out on getting a personal message from God! Nothing is more exciting.

Think about having a conversation with another person. You both speak and you both listen. The same is true with our conversations with the Lord when we're one-on-one with Him. We shouldn't be doing all the talking. God wants us to pour out our hearts to Him, and then He wants to respond to us. Jesus shared this parable:

> The gatekeeper opens the gate for him, and the sheep listen to his voice. He calls his own sheep by name and leads them out. When he has brought out all his own, he goes on ahead of them, and his sheep follow him because they know his voice (John 10:3-4).

Now let's reread these verses with some clarifying remarks added in:

> The gatekeeper [Jesus] opens the gate [a way for us to have direct communication with God] for him, and the sheep [you and me] listen to his voice. He [God] calls his own sheep by name [He speaks to us personally] and leads them out [providing us with direction]. When he has brought out all his own, he goes on ahead of them, and his sheep follow him because they know his voice [they know his voice because they have spent time with him] (John 10:3-4).

Jesus is the one who provides a way for us to be able to talk with God and hear from Him. God calls us by name. He wants to have a personal connection with each of us. Think about when you call someone's name. You know that person. You're calling on them so the two of you can connect in some way. And think about how great it is when people know and use *your* name. You feel included. If you've ever been the new girl at school or church, you know just what I mean. You walk around those first days and weeks with what feels like a flashing neon sign above your head letting everyone know you are lost, in need of a friend, and totally alone. And then when someone makes the effort to connect personally, it means everything. More than a few times I have felt a flood of relief when someone finally said, "Lysa, come sit with us."

When God calls us, it's even sweeter. These verses in John assure us that Jesus calls us by name, and He leads us with personal attention and care. The way God wants to connect with us is to provide direction for us in life. He's gone before us and sees the dangers and trials we will face. He is telling us the way to go, the perspectives to keep, the things to avoid, and the things to hold fast to. Most of all He is speaking to us because we are His own and He wants a relationship with us. He loves us, adores us, treasures us, and has a good plan for us. He longs for us to know His voice and listen to His voice. The only way to know and trust God in this way is to spend time with Him.

When we make the time to be with God, He will speak to us, and what we hear from Him in these quiet times will be echoed in other places. Listen for God's voice and then look for the message to be confirmed. If it is, you're ready to ask the fourth question.

Is What I'm Hearing Beyond Me?

When God leads or prompts us to do something small, we will be able to do it if we're willing. But sometimes God calls us to do something big, something we feel we can't do in our own strength because it is either beyond our ability or beyond our natural human desire. It is not something we can strategize and manipulate into being in and of ourselves. It can only happen by God's divine intervention. The beauty of doing things beyond ourselves is that we will know it was by God's doing and His alone. And to Him we give all the glory.

I remember when God called me to write my first book. It seemed so exciting and thrilling to think of accomplishing this huge life goal. I envisioned the cover with my name on it. I delighted in imagining the first time I would walk into a bookstore and quietly say to myself, "I wrote that." The excitement carried me through writing the first 10,000 words. Everything was clicking right along…until I got a note from my editor after she read my first installment. Her two-page, single-spaced feedback can be summed up in two shocking words: "Start over."

I got down on the floor beside my desk, buried my face in the carpet, and cried. "I can't do this, God. I can't write a whole book. What was I thinking? I'm not an author. I'm an imposter who somehow got lucky enough to fool this publisher with my proposal. But now they've seen the real me and think I'm a fool."

Did you notice an often-repeated word in my cries to God? "I'm not." "I can't." "I'm a fool." It was all about me and my inadequacies until I turned the statements into "God is." "God can." "God has called me; therefore, I am equipped."

If God is calling you to do something you feel is beyond you, you are in good company. God has a history of calling people to things that were beyond themselves. Pastor Rick Warren put it this way:

> Abraham was old, Jacob was insecure, Leah was unattractive, Joseph was abused, Moses stuttered, Gideon was poor, Samson was codependent, Rahab was immoral, David had an affair and all kinds of family problems, Elijah was suicidal, Jeremiah was depressed, Jonah was reluctant, Naomi was a widow, John the Baptist was eccentric to say the least, Peter was impulsive and hot-tempered, Martha worried a lot, the Samaritan woman had several failed marriages, Zachaeus was unpopular, Thomas had

doubts, Paul had poor health, and Timothy was timid. That's quite a group of misfits, but God used each of them in his service. He will use you too.[2]

This puts God's power into perspective, doesn't it? Don't look at your inabilities and dwell in your insecurities. Look at the Almighty God. Then take another look at that list of flawed people used by Him. Make the decision to give this difficult situation over to Him so that He will work in you and through you just like He did with every one of the people in this list (and millions of others who said yes). If you answer yes to the question *Is this beyond me?* chances are God is speaking.

Yes Factor

When you get into God's Word and let God's Word get into you, you'll discover His message for your life.

Would What I'm Hearing Please God?

It's easy to talk ourselves out of thinking we've heard from God. I think we'll pretty much use any excuse to convince ourselves it's not His voice so we don't need to act. When I was young and heard my mom calling me in for dinner, I would rationalize that the female voice coming from the general area of my house could *actually* be someone else's mom calling them in for chicken and green beans. I wanted to stay outside with my friends and enjoy the summer night. I'd dismiss her until I saw her coming down the street for me. Then I'd *believe* it was her. Then I'd know for certain it was time to obey.

It is so easy to start doing this with our heavenly parent as well. Soon we actually start to talk ourselves out of believing we ever really hear God's leading, but there's one very important question to ask when we feel prompted by Him to do something, one question that takes away our excuses: Would this please God? You see, if what you're doing pleases God, then even if what you thought you heard from Him wasn't His voice, you still please Him. We should always seek to err on the side of pleasing God. Ask this question, and you'll know what to do.

These five questions are your starting place. The more you practice listening for God's voice, the more it will become a natural part of your daily life. And here's the best news of all: God *wants* you to hear Him. He wants your faith to grow. He's told us so over and over in Scripture:

- This is my prayer: that your love may abound more and more in knowledge and depth of insight (Philippians 1:9).

- This is to my Father's glory, that you bear much fruit, showing yourselves to be my disciples (John 15:8).

- We ought always to thank God for you, brothers, and rightly so, because your faith is growing more and more, and the love all of you have for one another is increasing (2 Thessalonians 1:3).

- For this very reason, make every effort to add to your faith goodness; and to goodness, knowledge (2 Peter 1:5).

- As for other matters, brothers and sisters, we instructed you how to live in order to please God, as in fact you are living. Now we ask you and urge you in the Lord Jesus to do this more and more (1 Thessalonians 4:1).

You're Invited...
to Begin the Yes Adventure

WHAT:

An exciting adventure to discover God's amazing purpose and promises for you. The Yes adventure is personalized and powered for you by God.

WHEN:

It begins the moment you say "Yes, Lord!" You've opened the door to what is possible, now it is time to move forward in your extraordinary story.

WHERE:

It starts in your heart. The change happens within you and your spirit as you give your life to the exciting path of discovery and extraordinary faith.

WHAT TO BRING:

Gather these items for your faith journey through this book and beyond:

- Bible—if reading God's Word is new to you, choose a translation with a built-in commentary
- Journal
- Prayer list of your prayer needs and the prayer requests of others—make sure there is plenty of room to also list God's faithful answers
- Inspirational quotes or letters of encouragement from others
- Christian music, praise music, and other uplifting words

Living Out the Five Questions

My conversations with God are more than a spiritual exercise for me. They are a lifeline. In my early childhood, I did not have a dad who was very involved in my life. I was desperate to know I was loved. I remember watching other little girls with their dads and wondering what was so wrong with me that my dad didn't adore me the way theirs did. Maybe it was because I wasn't pretty enough. Maybe I wasn't smart enough. Maybe he had never wanted me. Have you asked these kinds of questions because someone in your life doesn't love you in a way you long to be loved?

I was blessed to have another man adopt me when my mom remarried. Charles has been a wonderful father to me who has loved me as his own. However, not having my biological father's love and acceptance left a hole in my heart. Often a little girl's sense of self-worth will be based on her father's love. And her opinion of God will often be based on her opinion of her earthly father.

Both of these were skewed for me. My sense of self-worth was severely lacking. I defined myself as an unwanted, unlovely, throwaway person. I viewed God as a distant, cold ruler who had somehow deemed me unworthy. Many years into my adult life, I came to see a different picture of God. He wooed me and loved me to a place where I finally surrendered my heart to Him.

Then a miracle happened...God redefined my identity.

I was no longer a throwaway child. I was a holy and dearly loved daughter of the Most High King. I truly became a brand-new creation. I found the love and acceptance that had been so lacking in my early childhood. That little girl in me craved to spend time with the daddy I had missed out on for so long. He whispered to my heart that I was pretty and special and smart, and, best of all, that I was loved.

Because I know what it feels like to be abandoned, I've always had a tender place in my heart for the orphaned child. But after having three biological daughters of my own, I brushed aside any notion of adopting. That was until one unsuspecting day when God connected my family with two teenage boys from the war-torn country of Liberia, Africa. This meeting changed my family forever as God so clearly whispered to our hearts that they were to become part of our family.

As soon as I heard His whisper, my mind raced through the five-question filter:

1. Does what I'm hearing line up with Scripture?
2. Is it consistent with God's character?
3. Is it being confirmed through messages I'm hearing at church or studying in my quiet times?
4. Is it beyond me?
5. Would it please God?

God is very clear in Scripture that as Christians we are to take care of widows and orphans. Just a few weeks before meeting the boys I recorded the following verse in my journal: "Religion that God our Father accepts as pure and faultless is this: to look after orphans and widows in their distress and to keep oneself from being polluted by the world" (James 1:27). I had no idea why I was drawn to write this verse in my journal, but God knew. He made sure I was familiar with an answer to my first filter question. Yes, adopting the boys absolutely lined up with Scripture. And in the same verse God answered the second question. God defines part of His character as "God our Father." I saw that God had been a Father to me in my time of need.

The confirmations were also undeniable. God had been bringing friends into my life who had adopted orphaned children. I never thought it would be something my husband would be open to, and yet God drew his heart to a place of acceptance. My girls begged us to consider adopting and prayed often for big brothers. It seemed everywhere I turned the theme of adopting was staring me in the face. Sermons at church, verses in my quiet times, songs on the radio, and whispers by God to my heart all seemed to be saying the same thing. Yes, adopting these boys was being confirmed.

The fourth question did not require much thought at all. I knew without a doubt this was totally beyond me. Having boys was beyond me. I had grown up with sisters and then had three daughters. I felt ill equipped to be a mom of boys—especially teenage boys. Having five kids was beyond me. My schedule was already crazy with three kids. How in the world would I be able to add two more? Financially, this seemed beyond what we could do. Not to mention the host of fears that flooded my brain. What if one of the boys hurt one of my girls or me or had emotional baggage that would take a huge toll on the stability of our family? I would only be willing to do this if I knew beyond a shadow of a doubt that it was God's plan and not my own. Only in His strength would this be possible.

The last question became the most important in our decision to pursue adopting the boys. More than anything else we desired to please God, but the pull of taking an easier path was incredible with this particular invitation. That's because the fear kicked in. The tug of belief that my worst fears would surely be waiting on the other side of this step of obedience made me want to run and hide. But the love of God kept my heart still, and His constant reassurances kept me on course. We said yes to God, not because we were completely comfortable with adopting, but rather because we completely trusted Him.

After the Yes

We let faith carry us as we faced the future as courageously as we could. We quoted Scripture after Scripture to remind ourselves that this was God's adventure and we were simply saying yes while trusting Him completely.

And you know what we discovered? Sheer joy. Not in the circumstances we faced necessarily, but in the absolute assurance we were being obedient to God and walking in the very center of His will.

On the other side of this great adoption adventure, I'm in awe of God's goodness. I can't imagine my life without these boys. I am so thankful I followed His perfect plan instead of being allured away by fear and worry. After years of happily being a mom to them, I'm more convinced that even though they were not born from my body, they were born from my heart. Maybe that was the purpose of that place in my heart that seemed so much like a hole when I was younger, but now I see it as the channel through which God brought my sons home.

I want to encourage you by confessing that listening for God's voice and communicating with Him has not always come naturally to me. These five filters have helped me draw closer to God and understand His voice and leading. I know they will make a difference in your daily conversation with Him. To this day I seek God's voice by asking for the desire, discipline, discernment, direction, and delight.

Have you ever asked God for this type of relationship with Him? When you ask for these things boldly and live in expectation of hearing from God, you will. I encourage you to

* Ask for the desire to want God more than anything else.

- Ask for the discipline to make your relationship with Him top priority.

- Ask for the discernment to know the difference between your thoughts and God's voice.

- Ask for God's direction as you make decisions and set your priorities.

- Ask for delight in your circumstances so that you may praise God in all things.

In Jeremiah 29:13 God promises, "You will seek me and find me when you seek me with all your heart." God does not hide from us. True to His character, He is present and available. He is saying "Yes, I am here for you." He is waiting for us each step of the way.

We can eagerly say yes to God with a trusting heart…because He has already said yes to us.

God's Word for You

Read Romans 12:1-2 in the NIV. Then, write out a definition for the following:

Living sacrifice:

Pleasing to God:

Do not conform:

The pattern of this world:

Transformed:

Renewing of your mind:

Test and approve God's will:

Summarize what you can learn from these verses about discerning God's voice:

List some areas of your life in which you currently honor God:

List some areas that you sense you may need to sacrifice or change:

Are there areas of your life where you've conformed to the world's way of thinking? How can you renew your mind in this area?

In The Message, Romans 9:25-26 says,

> "Hosea put it well: I'll call nobodies and make them some-bodies; I'll call the unloved and make them beloved. In the place where they yelled out, 'You're nobody!' they're calling you 'God's living children.'"

Paul continues,

> How can we sum this up? All those people who didn't seem interested in what God was doing actually embraced what God was doing as he straightened out their lives. And Israel, who seemed so interested in reading and talking about what God was doing, missed it. How could they miss it? Because instead of trusting God, they took over. They were absorbed in what they themselves were doing. They were so absorbed in their "God projects" that they didn't notice God right in front of them, like a huge rock in the middle of the road. And so they stumbled into him and went sprawling. Isaiah (again!) gives us the metaphor for pulling this together: Careful! I've put a huge stone on the road to Mount Zion, a stone you can't get around. But the stone is me! If you're looking for me, you'll find me on the way, not in the way (Romans 9:30-33 MSG).

God wants us to live in expectation of hearing from Him as He gives us directions or points us to a divine appointment. I pray you'll hear His glorious voice proclaiming, "You are somebody! You are my chosen beloved!"

Living Y.E.S. (Your Extraordinary Story)

Spend time writing in your journal about the times you have felt God working in your life. Also, pay attention to times when you've felt alone and sad. How does your view now of those times help you see God's hand in your situation?

List three times or ways God has made Himself known to you in your life. What aspect of His character did He reveal to you during these times?

1.

2.

3.

Change your negative thoughts by viewing the truth of God and the truth of who He is and what He can do through you. It is very powerful to gather your different "I'm nots" and "I can'ts" and give them to God as an offering to be transformed into great worth. Give your false thoughts the twist of truth to help you realize who God is and what He can do in your life right now. Write down a few of these here.

Example:

I'm not: good enough to resist temptation.

God is: strong enough to help me through this time of weakness.

I can't: pass this math test. I'm so bad at algebra.

God can: work good in situations through my faithfulness.

I'm not:

God is:

I can't:

God can:

. . . .

Describe a time when you have felt like a nobody. What have you learned about God that changes your view of yourself now?

. . . .

Do you sense God whispering to you, leading you, and speaking to you about a particular decision, circumstance, worry, need, or hope? Walk through the five-question filter here and discern His voice. Pray about and write down your answers:

1. Does what I'm hearing line up with Scripture?

2. Is it consistent with God's character?

3. Is it being confirmed through messages I'm hearing at church or studying in my quiet times?

4. Is it beyond me?

5. Would it please God?

Yes Prayer

Lord, lead me today. Help me walk through the questions I need to ask so that I am sure of Your voice and Your will. There's a lot of noise in my life. Sometimes it is hard to know which way to turn and which choice to make. I'm so glad I can turn to You, God. When I worry about making mistakes, You give me peace to move forward with faith and courage. You transform my imperfections by Your forgiveness, Your plan, and Your amazing purpose for my extraordinary story of yes. In Jesus' name, amen.

YES IN ACTION: LETTING GO

A Note from Hope's Yes Journey

It was my ninth birthday, and I had just been given a ten-dollar bill from my aunt. Like any girl, I do love the gifts that come with birthdays! I held that bill tightly in my hand as my family and I drove home from my aunt's house. Even as a young girl, I understood money offered me something. It was independence to go to a movie with a friend or buy something extra in the toy or candy aisle when I wanted it. So I stared at that bill and saw freedom.

You're doing the math and thinking, *Ten bucks? That wouldn't get her far!* But at this time in my life, it was a lot. And as I dreamed about what I might get with *my* cash, my mom burst my little bubble as she asked to borrow it! We were in the drive-through line to get lunch and she didn't have enough cash. She promised I'd get eight dollars in change and then she'd give me ones when we got home if only I'd release my hold of the ten.

"No." I shook my head and kept looking at my money.

My mom even offered to pay me several extra dollars if I'd help out right then. But my response was still a stubborn no. My reasoning was something like this: "Then I won't have a ten-dollar bill. I'll just have ones. I want to show my friends this!" Because the money was all I thought about, I rejected the chance to willingly, eagerly help my mom and be a girl who would say yes to God about things like money. Only when we pulled up to the payment window did the pressure get too great. I reluctantly gave my mom the money, but she had to pull it from my fingers.

She was disappointed and I knew it. Now I look back and think how God must've been disappointed as well by my resistance to giving. Mom was also sad because she knew that if I couldn't be faithful with that small bill, then I would not be ready for what was waiting for me at home.

You see, she knew what I didn't know…

My grandma had sent me a card with a *fifty*-dollar bill in it. That much more valuable piece of cash was waiting in a stack of cards for me on our kitchen table. My mom didn't tell me that because she wanted me to let go of my money on my own and to do it as an act of compassion and kindness, not because I knew I'd score more money later.

My mom has shared this story with others, and when I hear it I want to hide. But I've learned another faith lesson from her—it's really important to share our imperfect moments with one another as part of the yes journey. If we all pretend to be perfect, we're never real with one another, and we aren't able to later represent God's strength through us in a real way.

I've learned I have to release my hold on the world's promises, riches, and lies and choose to embrace the God-things before the very cool yes journey begins. I'm sure there are times my mom looks at me now and sees me shake my head defiantly about something just like that day years ago. But each year, each day, I am learning God has greater things in store than anything I hold onto with a tight fist and selfish attitude.

I've shared one of my embarrassing moments that became a faith lesson. Now it's your turn. Journal or tell a friend about a time when you were stubborn and unwilling to release something to God. Have you ever made a new outfit, your selfish demands, or your popularity more important than God or God's leading? Maybe you are even dealing with something like that now.

We are not nine years old anymore. We've grown in many ways. For one thing, I hope we're taller! But I also hope that you and I are willing and eager to let go of the unimportant stuff so that we can receive the extraordinary gifts, challenges, and dreams God has for us. It's not easy to be a young woman who says yes to God, but it's so worth it. Grow with me toward yes.

Hope

3

God Wants Your Heart

Have you ever had a chance to give in a big way to someone, to God, or even to a passionate pursuit but at the last minute you held back instead of going all out? I've done this before…too many times to count. But the real eye-openers were the times I've been on the receiving end of people who only gave a teeny bit of themselves through time and kindness when I longed for them to be committed and fully attentive. Those times made me feel "less than" and unimportant, and they helped me to realize how God must feel when I don't give Him my undivided heart. I had an experience that revealed to me the importance and the joy of giving God what He deserves—everything.

I was attending a large conference at which the speaker challenged us to pray and ask God to use us in an extraordinary way for His kingdom. Something stirred in my heart, and I started praying. When I got back to the hotel room that evening, I not only continued to pray for God to use me, but I wanted Him to show me what He required. I knew I couldn't climb to new heights in my spiritual journey without submitting my entire life and heart to His purpose, so I knelt beside my hotel bed to ask God to reveal to me what to do.

After I finished praying, I picked up the remote control to click on the evening news and two words suddenly came to mind: radical obedience. *Radical obedience?* I questioned. *I'm obedient, Lord. I read my Bible, go to church, and try to be a good person.* Then something else came to my mind: *Stop watching TV altogether and put your house up for sale.*

What? I was stunned. *God, how do I know this is You speaking and not just a crazy notion in my head?*

One thing I did know—I was at a crossroads. I could brush aside these thoughts and say I didn't know for sure this was God speaking to me, or I could follow His direction. I put down the remote and dropped to my knees once again. I wanted to do whatever He asked me to do, but I wasn't sure I could do this. I didn't doubt God. I doubted my ability to really know if He was speaking to me. I doubted my courage. I mean, how could I have the guts to follow through with what felt like a drastic, quick decision to throw out my television and put a "For Sale" sign on my lawn?

As I continued to pray, my mind was flooded with Scriptures consistent with what I felt God was calling me to do. One powerful portion of Scripture was 1 Peter 1:13-16:

> With minds that are alert and fully sober, set your hope fully on the grace to be brought to you when Jesus Christ is revealed at his coming. As obedient children, do not conform to the evil desires you had when you lived in ignorance. But just as he who called you is holy, so be holy in all you do; for it is written: "Be holy, because I am holy."

I decided it must be God I was hearing from and I should look for His confirmation over the next couple of weeks.

I also asked God why He'd chosen these two specific actions. After all, I wasn't a TV junkie, and our house didn't have us living beyond our means. As I prayed, I felt Him telling me why the TV had to go. I enjoyed sitting down after an exhausting day and being entertained. God showed me I was vulnerable and empty during those times. It wasn't that what I was watching was bad— it just wasn't His best. I was filling myself with the world's perspectives and influences, while He wanted to be my strength and fill me with Himself. I knew it would be hard to break this habit, but I was determined to ask God for the strength to do so. I prayed that my desire to please Him would be stronger than my desire for television.

I hope you understand I'm *not* saying all television is bad, and I'm not making a case here for all Christians to throw out their sets. I know you probably have a list of shows you love and look forward to watching and then talking about with friends. I completely understand that television can be a source of pleasure and even connection. But what I am saying is that God wanted *my* obedience in this area for a certain season. I actually had felt His leading to turn off the TV before that night in the hotel room, but I had ignored Him and justified my disobedience to the point where God needed to get my attention. He wanted me to make a choice between my desire and His.

And guess what? I took a break from television for two and a half years. When I finally felt God giving me the freedom to turn it back on, something amazing had happened. I was no longer tied to it. I no longer felt the need to record programs I missed. I no longer had any must-see shows. I was able to objectively and carefully discern what would be good to watch and what wouldn't. I found I was much pickier than I'd ever been before and a lot less willing to make compromises on what was questionable. God may not ask you to turn off the TV or disconnect from online shows and Facebook—but He may ask you to do something else. The point here is there will come a time in your life when you will need to decide between your will and His. Pay attention to what God is asking you to let go of or what He is pointing out to be an obstacle in your life that keeps your attention away from Him and is distracting you from living your extraordinary story.

God Is Preparing You

Remember how God had nudged me to turn off the television even before I was fully aware of what He was asking me to do on a bigger scale? Think about the recent times God has prompted you to do something. Could these prompts be a preview of something bigger He is asking you to do? Spend some time thinking about that as you go through this chapter. I'm excited about the great dreams and possibilities that await you as soon as you connect God's leading with your extraordinary story.

Each prompt from God is part of His preparation plan. He prepares our hearts, the events we will be a part of, and the ways His message will come to us through different avenues. We don't want to miss the prompts because they are far more significant than they may seem at the time.

One thing you can be assured of is that God has already worked out all the details of what your obedience will accomplish—and it is good. We need not fear what our obedience will cause to happen in our life. We should only fear what our *dis*obedience will cause us to miss.

The sooner this truth resonates in your heart, the quicker you can make peace with a command from God you don't fully understand. We tend to want to see the big picture complete with all the details before stepping out in obedience to God. We want to get a confirmation email listing what we'd be giving up and what we'd be gaining so we could compare, think it over, post it on our blog and ask for input from friends, and *then* decide if the trade is worth it.

This is how I felt about God's request to sell our home. I kept thinking, *Why would God ask me to let this go?* My home is very precious to me. Not for its financial value, but for the wealth of memories we have made there. I thought about the things we would not be able to take with us if the house sold: the door frame where we've measured each of our girls' growth since they were toddlers, the handprint tiles we made when we added a bathroom in the playroom, the Bible we'd buried in the foundation when we built the house. Small as they are, these things made our house our home. I decided I would wait for God's confirmation that we were really supposed to put the house on the market.

When I returned home from the conference, I was nervous about mentioning selling the house to my husband, Art, so I said very little. I just kept looking and listening for God's confirmation. I asked Him to reveal the perfect time to share my heart with my husband. A few days later we were both in our bedroom reading when Art looked up from his book and told me about the devotion he'd just studied.

"It had to do with the fact that sometimes we work so hard to make a heaven on earth that our hearts are pulled away from our real home with God," he said. Then he looked me straight in the eyes and added, "Lysa, I think we should sell our house."

No kidding. Isn't that amazing? I can promise you that once you give God your whole heart and your undivided attention, these amazing moments are not only possible, they are probable. That's how incredible our God is.

Even though I had prayed about this, I was shocked when Art's words confirmed the very thing God had shared with me. After a silent moment of pure awe at God's incredible way of confirming

His message, I told my husband I would call a real estate agent right away.

When we got to the meeting with the real estate agent, she asked all kinds of questions about the house and our land. When the pond was mentioned, Art's eyes sparkled and he went into great detail about all he'd done to make it the perfect bass pond. He talked on and on about it, and he even went so far as to say that while we wanted to be obedient to God in putting the house on the market, we really didn't want to try to aggressively sell it.

We left the meeting and headed home. When we reached the part of our driveway that curves around the pond, we were stunned by what we saw—82 dead fish floating in the water. We'd never seen even one dead fish in our pond, so seeing 82 stopped us in our tracks. What followed was a scene I'll never forget. Art got out of the car and, with tears streaming down his cheeks, knelt beside the pond to ask for the Lord's forgiveness. God had made His request clear, and we had given Him a halfhearted response.

A Whole and Purified Heart

God is not interested in half of our heart. He wants it all, and He wants to remove the things standing in the way of that.

> "I will send my messenger, who will prepare the way before me. Then suddenly the Lord you are seeking will come to his temple; the messenger of the covenant, whom you desire, will come," says the LORD Almighty. But who can endure the day of his coming? Who can stand when he appears? For he will be like a refiner's fire or a launderer's soap. He will sit as a refiner and purifier of silver; he will purify the Levites and refine them like gold and silver (Malachi 3:1-3).

The messenger in this passage refers to John the Baptist. He would go before Jesus and prepare for Jesus' first coming. Now *we* are the messengers who are called to prepare people for Jesus' second coming. God wants to purify our whole heart so we are prepared and mature for our calling.

God turns up the heat from the refiner's fire so our impurities will rise to the top, where they can be skimmed off and discarded. Have you done an advanced workout for a school sport or at home on a Wii system? Put in an hour workout of power Pilates, dancing, or soccer, and you know exactly what the "burn" feels like. You also know how great it feels to sweat the impurities out of your body. Just as it takes some heat to refine our bodies, it also takes heat to refine our spirits.

I appreciate the insight the *Life Application Study Bible* sheds on this passage:

> Without this heating and melting, there could be no purifying. As the impurities are skimmed off the top, the reflection of the worker appears in the smooth, pure surface. As we are purified by God, his reflection in our lives will become more and more clear to those around us. God says leaders (here the Levites) should be especially open to his purification process.[1]

It's interesting that the Bible also tells us that the Levites' inheritance would not be land but rather God Himself (Numbers 18:20). God wants us to desire Him above all else.

I didn't want to give God any more halfhearted answers. I was determined that when He spoke to my heart, He would never again have to shout. By asking Art and me to put our home up for sale, God was skimming greed from our hearts. We were holding what He had given us with a closed fist. God wanted to teach us that when we tightly hold on to the things of this world, we not only lose the desire to give, but we lose the ability to receive more as well.

Did you catch that? If we hold all that we treasure with our hands open and our palms facing upward, we are telling God we recognize it is His and we offer it up freely to Him. He may or may not remove what we've offered Him, but He will continue to fill our open hands with blessings—His amazing blessings and not the cheap counterfeits of the world!

Yes Factor

Radical obedience has the power to ignite your God-given potential.

Giving It All to God

No one understands the concept of offering it all to God better than Abraham (Genesis 22:1-19). Read these verses because they have all the amazing elements of an incredible, true story: drama, suspense, action, and a surprising twist. When God commanded Abraham to lay his only son on the altar of obedience, I am sure Abraham fully expected to plunge the dagger into Isaac. It would be an end...the death of a dream. Yet, Abraham was willing to give up the son he loved to the God who loved him more, and God blessed him. God poured His compassion and mercy into Abraham's open hands, and He spared Isaac. But even more than that, God lavished the evidence of His presence upon Abraham, and Abraham walked away having experienced God in a way few ever do. God wants to know if we're willing to give up what we love to Him who loves us more. He desires for us to open our fists and trust Him with absolutely everything.

As I opened my fist about our home, I felt God piercing a dark little corner of my heart. My selfishness couldn't reflect His generous heart. But as I let His light in, His reflection became clearer in my life. Then something amazing came about. Just as God provided a ram instead of taking Isaac, God did not allow our house to sell. For more than a year the Realtor's lockbox stayed on our front door as a beautiful reminder that we were managers and not owners of our home. Interestingly enough, the week we brought our boys home the box disappeared. Maybe the Realtor finally came and got it or maybe God removed it to get our attention. But isn't the timing interesting?

I'm so thankful I made the connection between these two events so I could weather the transition of going from three to five children in a more settled way. I've always been a bit particular with my home. I like it to smell nice, feel peaceful, and have a sense of order about it. Having three little girls who liked to play quietly fit so nicely into my scope of how things should be. Then suddenly we had five children and things stopped being just so. It's not that any one of us is particularly messy or loud; it's just the nature of seven people living under the same roof.

A girl likes her space. Am I right? We enjoy making our room our own and creating something that reflects our personality and style. I felt like this about my entire house. I loved having it be clean, orderly, and inviting. To me, this order was a way for me to better care for my family and for visitors alike. My home was my refuge. What's wrong with that? Well, I'll tell you how that can become a problem. Every time I cleaned something that ended up dirty minutes later, I felt a little pang in my heart. Every time I hunted for an item that had mysteriously disappeared from its assigned place, I felt this pang twist and grow. Every time I discovered something broken, it felt as though the pang had grown into a choking vine in my throat. I found myself snapping at my family and blaming them for anything and everything that went wrong at home.

One day I was in the middle of one of my aggravated search and rescue pursuits of a missing item when one of my sons stopped me and asked me the strangest question. "Mom, will you teach me to dance?"

I was grumpy, on a mission, and in no mood to dance. My thoughts were racing. *Dance? Dance? I am trying to teach you to put things back where they belong and stop messing up my house, and you want to dance?* Then my attention turned fully to him as he lifted out his hands, signaling he wanted to dance as if I were wearing a princess ball gown and he were wearing a tux. His gaze was so sincere that suddenly the missing scissors I had been so frustrated by no longer gnawed at my attention. Here was this beautiful young man awkwardly lifting up his arms and asking me to dance. This boy, who just months before had been stuck in a forgotten orphanage on the other side of the world with no hope and no reason to dance, was standing in my kitchen asking me to show him how.

I took his hand, wrapped my arm around his shoulder, and taught him to step and glide and twirl and dip. The world seemed to melt away as I realized what a privilege this experience was. How selfish of me to call our home "my house." How ungrateful I must have seemed to God. I could have a neat and tidy house where things never got lost, misplaced, or broken if there were no others living there but me, but my heart never wanted just a house. My heart longs for a home full of people whom I love. As we stopped dancing, I lifted up a prayer of thanksgiving to God. I praised Him for teaching me to finally let go of my house so I could have a real home.

I no longer see things like this in my life as mere coincidence and brush them aside. I take a closer look at these events and encounters. I pray over them. I ask God what I'm supposed to learn through the experience.

What moments have you had like this? The kind where you are certain that God's fingerprints are all over them. Live in expectation of experiencing God and hearing His voice. Record these times in a journal. Look for answers to the prayers you've prayed and understanding from the steps of obedience and faithfulness God has called you to take. See how He weaves everything together in wonderful ways.

Living in the Sweet Secret Place

Do you ever feel like things are closing in on you? Do you wish you could step away from stress and life's concerns? In the middle of a crazy day at school, wouldn't it be nice to put life on pause?

I want to let you in on something.

There is a place I escape to that allows my soul to breathe and rest and reflect. It is the place where I can drop the "yuck" the world hands me and trade it in for the fullness of God. It is where God reassures me, confirms He has everything under control, and gives me a new filter through which I can process life. The Bible calls it the remaining place. I call it my sweet secret place.

John 15:4 says, "Remain in me, as I will remain in you. No branch can bear fruit by itself; it must remain in the vine. Neither can you bear fruit unless you remain in me." Let's be honest. It's hard for a well-meaning soul who desires radical obedience to God to live in a body made of flesh. Our flesh is pulled by the distractions of the world, lured to sell our soul for temporary pleasures and conned by Satan's evil schemes. Other people rub us the wrong way, and we instantly want to give them a piece of our mind. Worldly wealth screams that if only you could do more to have more, then ultimate happiness could be yours. And our right to be right seems to supersede the sacrificial call of God. All the while He invites our souls to break away from the world and remain in Him.

To remain in Him and enter the secret place, I simply have to close my eyes and make the choice to be with God.

Sometimes it's because I'm in a desperate place. I pray, "God, I am here and I need You right now. I'm feeling attacked, invaded, pressed, and stressed. Meet me here and help me process what I'm facing using Your truth. Nothing more and nothing less. I don't want this thing I'm facing to be processed through my selfish and insecure flesh. I will surely act in a displeasing and dishonoring way if I'm left to face this on my own. Block my flesh's natural reaction and fill me with Your Spirit. You handle this for me. You speak what needs to be spoken and give power to hold my tongue for what needs to be left in silence."

Other times I need to be with God because I'm feeling pulled into something I know is not part of His best plan for me. I see something new I can't afford. How easy it is to justify getting a new jacket, pair of shoes, or bag that's perfect for school. When we play the justification game in our minds, it's really easy to decide to deal with the consequences later. Can you think of a few times you've done this recently? Another big area of compromise for some girls is in relationships. Maybe it is a relationship we know is not in God's will but we pursue it or stay involved anyway. Another area that can lure us into bad habits—food. We might have a few snack or meal favorites that aren't very healthy, or maybe we just aren't good at stopping when we are full.

Whatever it is, we don't have to be powerless against this pull. We can pray, "God, I know You are more powerful than this desire. I know this thing I want so much will only provide temporary pleasure. I know the consequences of making this choice will rob my joy and peace in the near future. Through Your power I am making the choice to walk away. I will find my delight in You and look forward to feeling Your fullness replace the emptiness this desire is creating."

Still other times I simply know I need a fresh filling of God's Spirit in me. I go to this secret place and simply talk to God. Then I listen for His voice. Sometimes He provides direction and instruction on something that needs to be done. Other times I sense Him warning me of something coming. Still other times He simply lavishes me with His love.

I love saying yes to God and going to the secret place with Him. He clearly tells us in John 15:4 that this is the only way to bear fruit in our lives. It is the only way to experience what Galatians 5:22-23 explains this fruit to be: love, joy, peace, forbearance, kindness, goodness, faithfulness, gentleness, and self-control. Oh, how I want these to be the character of my heart and the legacy of my life.

You're Invited...
to Experience the Sweet Secret Place

WHAT:
Develop intimate communication with God, and you will experience the peaceful refuge of His comfort, safety, assurances, and love.

WHEN:
Throughout the day and whenever you want to be in God's presence is the moment to be in the secret place. There isn't a time that you are separated from God. Lift up your prayer, whisper His name. He will hear you all day, every day.

WHERE:

Wherever you are is the place to call on God and experience that secret place of closeness with your Lord. Anywhere the walls seem to be closing in on you—school, home, a friend's house—that's where and when you'll want the peace of God's presence.

WHAT TO BRING:

An open, loving heart and a willingness to listen. Bring your deep desire to be known and loved unconditionally.

When Yes Is Your First and Final Answer

The more we say yes to God, the more we will live in expectation of seeing Him. The more we expect to see Him, the more we will. The more you experience Him, the more you'll trust Him. The more you trust Him, the more you'll open up your hands and heart in absolute faithfulness to receive what He is offering, saying, asking, or requiring.

In other words, obedience is the key that unlocks the secret place with God. John 15:10 goes on to explain this: "If you obey my commands, you will remain in my love." Obedience and faithfulness become extraordinary when we say, "Yes, God, whatever You want," and mean it. Can you say this to your parents? When you've been asked by a friend or family member if you'd do them a favor, have you responded with great eagerness *before* you've heard what the request is? Not many of us can answer yes to that. God is calling us to take such a leap of faith and faithfulness for Him.

But how do we do this?

How do we leave behind the way we've always done things?

How do we risk such vulnerability before the Lord when we've been trying to become independent and strong individuals?

We release our grip on all that we love and offer it back to Him. Why? Because He loves us more than anyone else. Because He loves us more than we even know to love ourselves. And because He plants in us the wonder of lasting joy and purpose—something a new bracelet or technology upgrade can never do. Do you realize what happens when you release your grip on what you love? Your upturned, empty hands are then open and able to receive the blessings that God will pour out—His abundant, unexpected, radical blessings. Soon, saying yes to God will no longer be a discipline of your heart but rather the center of your life.

God's Word for You

Titus 2:11-14 in The Message says,

> God's readiness to give and forgive is now public. Salvation's available for everyone! We're being shown how to turn our backs on a godless, indulgent life, and how to take on a God-filled, God-honoring life. This new life is starting right now, and is whetting our appetites for the glorious day when our great God and Savior, Jesus Christ, appears. He offered himself as a sacrifice to free us from a dark, rebellious life into this good, pure life, making us a people he can be proud of, energetic in goodness.

What area of your life is excessive or self-serving instead of godly? Ask for God's forgiveness and His strength as you turn your back on these areas and move toward His will.

Is there an area God might be leading you to give up either permanently or for a season?

What is holding you back from doing this?

Read Isaiah 41:13. Are we to give things up in our own strength? Are we walking this new path of deeper obedience alone?

List the fruit of the Spirit found in the secret abiding place (Galatians 5:22-23).

Which three fruit of the Spirit do you want to focus on when you experience that sweet time with God?

1.

2.

3.

Living Y.E.S. (Your Extraordinary Story)

When you think about God calling you by name, how does that make you feel?

What circumstance or need do you want to give to God today? In prayer, written or spoken, ask Him to speak to you by name and to guide you in this personal area. Journal about what it means to be able to call on God by name every day and in all things.

What does this statement mean to you now that you've journeyed through this chapter? "We need not fear what our obedience will cause to happen in our life. We should only fear what our *dis*obedience will cause us to miss."

What excites you about this statement in Titus 2:12: "This new life is starting right now"? Why is a new beginning in God so important to you?

Yes Prayer

God, You know me by name and You call on me and my heart today. It is such a gift that You care about my day, my life, and my hopes and dreams. Today I ask for help to let go of certain areas of my life that are not pleasing to You. Shed light on my actions, thoughts, or longings that do not line up with Your big hope for me, Lord. I give to You each one of those so that I can have open hands to receive Your blessings and to pass them along to others as You lead me to do. When I wake up each morning, I will find strength and purpose in knowing that You love me and have a hope for me. I will listen for Your voice, Lord. In Jesus' name, amen.

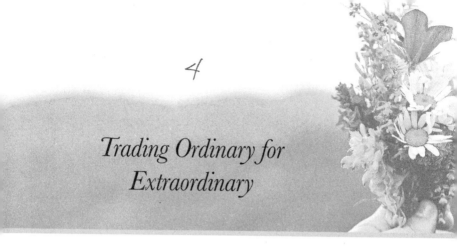

4

Trading Ordinary for Extraordinary

Our journey to becoming a young woman who says yes to God starts with Jesus. It is His amazing love that compels us to live righteous, transformed lives, and His sacrifice and grace allows us to do this.

> Christ's love compels us, because we are convinced that one died for all, and therefore all died. And he died for all, that those who live should no longer live for themselves but for him who died for them and was raised again. So from now on we regard no one from a worldly point of view. Though we once regarded Christ in this way, we do so no longer. Therefore, if anyone is in Christ, the new creation has come: the old has gone, the new is here! All this is from God, who reconciled us to himself through Christ and gave us the ministry of reconciliation (2 Corinthians 5:14-18).

Being obedient is not our way of earning God's favor. It is not the path to a more prosperous life. God's favor is with those who love His Son, and our promise of prosperity lies in what we have waiting for us in our eternal home.

Jesus, whose amazing love compels us, said, "If you hold to

my teaching, you are really my disciples. Then you will know the truth and the truth will set you free" (John 8:31-32). The truth is the name of Jesus that causes us to pause and redefine ourselves. The love compels us to embrace the calling to be Jesus' ambassador. Christ's love motivates us to be a disciple and fills us with a longing to know the truth. The truth is the freedom to soar above this life and learn to live beyond ourselves and our circumstances.

The real question now becomes do we really want this freedom, this life of purpose that now lies before us? Are we willing to be interrupted in the middle of our busy lives to see God, hear God, and pursue God? Do we want to be compelled by the love of Christ to serve Him and others? Do we really want a Lord of all of our life?

The Power to Obey

If Christ is the very source of radical obedience, and it is His love that compels us, then it is His power that enables us to do what we're called to do.

Know this: Satan will do everything he can to convince you to say no to God. Satan's name means "one who separates." He wants to separate you from God's best by offering what seems "very good" from a worldly perspective. He wants you to deny Christ's power in you. He wants to distract you from God's radical purpose for you.

The apostle John warned us of Satan's strategic plan:

> Do not love the world or anything in the world. If anyone loves the world, love for the Father is not in them. For everything in the world—the lust of the flesh, the lust of the eyes, and the pride of life—comes not from the Father but from the world (1 John 2:15-16).

The *Life Application Bible* offers this insight:

> Some people think that worldliness is limited to external behavior—the people we associate with, the places we go, the activities we enjoy. Worldliness is also internal because it begins in the heart and is characterized by three attitudes: 1. the cravings of the sinful man—preoccupation with gratifying physical desires; 2. the lust of his eyes—craving and accumulating things, bowing down to the god of materialism; and 3. boasting of what he has and does—obsession of one's status or importance…By contrast, God values self-control, a spirit of generosity, and a commitment to humble service. It is possible to give the impression of avoiding worldly pleasures while still harboring worldly attitudes in your heart.[1]

It all began with Eve. She had God's best and traded it all because Satan convinced her that worldly good was more appealing and worth the swap: "When the woman saw that the fruit of the tree was good for food [physical need: the lust of the flesh] and pleasing to the eye [psychological need: the lust of the eyes], and also desirable for gaining wisdom [emotional need: the pride of life], she took some and ate it [sin separated man from God's best]" (Genesis 3:6). The rest of Genesis 3 covers the shame, hiding, blaming, punishment, and banishment from the Garden.

This story doesn't end in Genesis 3. Jesus came and everything changed. He faced temptation just like Eve: "Jesus was led by the Spirit into the desert to be tempted by the devil" (Matthew 4:1). And He was tempted in the same three ways Eve was tempted, only Jesus' temptations were magnified a hundredfold. Eve was in a lush garden with delicious food, an incredible companion, and all the comforts of paradise. Jesus had been in a desert for 40 days, where He went without food, companionship, or comfort of any sort.

Satan tempted Him with food outside of God's plan for someone who was fasting (physical need: the lust of the flesh), an opportunity to prove Himself (emotional need: the pride of life), and the riches of the world (psychological need: lust of the eyes). Jesus withstood the temptations because instead of taking His eyes off of God, He intentionally focused on God and refuted each of Satan's temptations by quoting God's Word.

Satan has no new tricks up his sleeve. He still has nothing better to tempt us with than worldly things. Physical, emotional, and psychological pleasures that fall outside the will of God are still what Satan is using to pull the hearts of God's people away.

For me, the most amazing part of looking at Eve's temptation in relation to Jesus' temptation is what happens next in each of their lives. Eve turns away from God and says yes to worldly distractions. The next chapter of her life is tragic. Eve has two sons, one of whom kills the other. Jesus turns to God and says yes to His divine plan. The next chapter of His life is triumphant. Jesus begins His ministry here on earth. Something will happen next in our life as well. Will the next page in your life be filled with doubts and distractions? Or will it be filled with discovering the blessing of answering God's call on your life?

Read a selection from this amazing yes journey journal entry and discover how Christine longed to go from ordinary to extraordinary in her faith and how she followed God toward extraordinary faith.

> Ever since I became a Christian in high school, the mark of my faith had always been radical obedience to Christ. I loved the church and everything about it, and I was always striving to follow Jesus beyond the everyday practicalities of faith. I was always certain there had to be more to Christianity than just Bible study, fellowship times, and prayer, and I found true joy in being involved in the lives around me.

In the aftermath of September 11, though, I found myself with new questions, seeking God's true direction. I found myself disillusioned with the church and disenchanted with my faith. I heard Lysa speak at a women's conference, and it was as though my heart was being called back to the roots of the radical obedience she was talking about.

As I celebrated my birthday the other week, I really had a chance to reflect on where God has been taking me over the past year. Has it ever been a wild ride! He has torn down all the things I had held so dearly about the church and about Christianity. I am finding the Jesus I knew when I first became a Christian—the Jesus of social justice, mercy, and compassion. The Jesus who did not walk blindly through the earth without feeling the suffering of those around Him. He and the disciples were not tame and safe. They were not a social club with watered-down grace and entry requirements that have nothing to do with the sacred. They did not trade that which was eternal for that which was material.

At the same time, God has reawakened a heart of compassion and mercy in me. I am more aware than ever of the needs of others, and I have found great joy in working with social projects and even acts of compassion in everyday life. I see so much brokenness, so much pain in the lives of the women around me, and so often their cries are unheard and their needs go unnoticed as they walk alone. I have been trying to reach out more to those around me and to draw them closer to the only One who holds the answers to life's questions.

I've discovered it's so simple to bring the light of God into the midst of our everyday world. It is in the small acts of life that He can be reflected so beautifully—taking a meal to a new mother, welcoming a new neighbor with an invitation for dinner, or even just smiling at strangers as we pass them on the street. As I pause to help others, I am reminded that, just like

Jesus, we are called to notice the people around us and to bring a touch of hope into their lives.

Looking back at where I've been, I can see now that I had gotten off track. I was caught up in the social club mentality that so often permeates the church, and I had lost sight of what was really important. Yet, out of my brokenness I have seen the true call of Christ…a call to love our neighbors in ways that may seem radical in our selfish, sin-soaked culture. It has been a definite reawakening for me, a challenge to throw off the status quo and to really make a difference in my world. I am convinced that this is a picture of the true church…not a forced sort of family bonding because we all sit in the same building on Sunday, but a true family built out of genuine love for one another. And in those relationships, Christ's love is so evident and so full.

In following the path of radical obedience, I have tasted the mystery of the sacred fellowship that comes when two or more are gathered in His name, and it has added a richness to my life I would never again want to live without. It is a richness that goes beyond the tradition of the church to a holy existence before a dangerous and untamed God. It is an invitation to live tremblingly joyful before the God of radical obedience and radical grace, the God I want to know and serve all the days of my life.

Christine has discovered the joy of a heart wholly committed to God. She has discovered there is no end to what God can do with you—if you let Him.

Where True Change Comes From

How did Christine do it? What changed her walk of faith from ordinary to extraordinary?

Perhaps the better question to ask is *who* changed her walk of faith from ordinary to extraordinary? When we answer that question, we find the true source of radical obedience, and our soul transcends the pitfalls of everyday life that keep us from all God has for us.

Radical obedience is not just following a list of right things to do. Nonbelievers can do that and call it "good." Radical obedience is choosing to exchange what is "right" for God's righteousness. Only the pursuit of God's righteousness leads to His best. And it's there we find the source: "God made him who had no sin to be sin for us, so that in him we might become the righteousness of God" (2 Corinthians 5:21).

The answer is simple and complicated at the same time: It's Jesus. He is our source. He should be the only object of our pursuit. When we accept Jesus Christ as Lord of our life, we exchange our worthless sin for the immeasurable worth of His righteousness.

The apostle Peter put it this way: "In your hearts revere Christ as Lord" (1 Peter 3:15). He must be Lord of all if He is our Lord at all. Many people know Christ as their Savior, but when you and I say yes to God, we are responding to know Him as Lord. He becomes Guide, Ruler, and Leader of your heart. A young woman willing and intent on following God's will is able to take time to reach out to others, even when we have crazy busy days. The obedient soul redefines who she is through God's eyes, and any hesitation to do what He asks fades away.

Going All-In As a Believer

Life can present many opportunities for each of us to feel that we're called to perform well rather than *live* our faith in an extraordinary way. When have you stressed over your performance or success more than you have rested in God? When have you tried to be someone you aren't just to fit in for a moment, a day…for years? Most of us do this more often than we care to admit.

God wants us to get some things settled in our heart, and deciding whether we are all-in is one of those. Do we want to chase after the world's empty measure of value instead of His fullness? Or do we want our lives to be characterized by perfect love instead of perfect performance? Many people halfheartedly claim to be Christians, believing that because we will never be perfect this side of eternity we have an excuse to pursue that which pleases our human longings. Why not push the limits, live for the now, and worry about eternity later? The problem is that we miss the whole point of our existence, the very purpose for which we were created. God made us for the relationship of His perfect love. While we are not capable of perfect performance this side of eternity, we are capable of perfect love. We can settle in our hearts that we will choose God's love and the pursuit of a love relationship with Him above all else, no matter what comes our way.

Yes Factor

Exchange a halfhearted life for a wholehearted faith. Give God your all.

The day my husband and I made this decision we were in the hospital with our middle daughter, who was then six weeks old. She had seemed a perfectly healthy baby until an allergic reaction to the protein in my breast milk landed us in the intensive care unit. The doctors told us on the fourth day of our visit that Ashley needed emergency surgery, and they did not expect her to survive. They gave us five minutes to tell our baby goodbye.

My heart was shattered. I so desperately wanted to scoop her up and run out of the hospital. I wanted to somehow breathe my life into hers. I wanted to take her place. I could handle my own death so much easier than the death of my child. Art prayed over

Ashley, we both said our goodbyes, and then, with tears streaming down our faces, we let her go.

Art took me outside to the hospital parking lot, where I collapsed into his arms. He gently cupped my face in his hands and reminded me that Ashley was God's child to give and His to take back. "Lysa, God loves Ashley even more than we do," he gently told me. "We must trust His plan."

Art then asked me to do something, and it changed my whole perspective on my relationship with God: "We have to get it settled in our hearts that we will love God no matter the outcome of Ashley's surgery."

At first I resented his desire that we love God in this way. I feared it might give God the impression it was okay to take Ashley. With all my being I wanted to hold on to my child and refuse God. Yet, though I was heartbroken, I also felt God's compassion. I felt Him drawing me close. He knew firsthand the pain we were feeling because He'd felt it Himself. I knew that, ultimately, I had no ability to control my child's future. With tears pouring from our eyes, Art and I released our sweet Ashley to the Lord and promised to love Him no matter what.

It was as if the more I fell into God's arms, the less the pain of the moment seared my heart. Feeling the power of God took away the fear of the unknown. I stopped thinking about the what-ifs and let my soul simply say, *Okay. God, in this minute I choose rest with You and in You. I will not let my mind go to the minutes that are coming. I will simply be in this moment and face it with peace.*

That day we settled our love for God not just for this situation but for all time. Though we didn't feel at all happy, a gentle covering of unexplainable joy settled over our hearts. Knowing that the One who loved Ashley even more than we did was taking care of her, and that His plan for her was perfect, brought peace in the middle of heartbreak.

The end of this chapter of Ashley's life was miraculous and wonderful. Though the doctors can't explain how, she made a full recovery. Who can understand why God answers prayer the way He does? We just know we're grateful. And we can also know that no matter God's answer, our hearts were settled to trust and love Him. This kind of radical obedience brings about a depth of relationship with God you can't get any other way.

Have you faced a time when God has asked you to rest in Him no matter the outcome? Chances are, this has happened more often than you know. If you've ever been anxious about a test or a school project, He has longed for you to rest in Him. If you've stayed up late at night worried about your family and how they are getting along, He has been there to hold you and to hold the trouble you face. No matter what—God is with us. And no matter what—we are to rest in Him.

Nothing in life is certain. Circumstances roll in and out like the ocean's tide. The unknown can seem so frightening as we ponder all the tragic possibilities we know can and do happen to people. We catch ourselves wondering what the next page of life might hold. We can't stop or control the things that roll our way any more than we can stop the water's edge, but we can make the minute-by-minute choice to let our souls rest in God.

> Rest knowing all is so safe in My Hands. Rest is Trust. Ceaseless activity is distrust. Without the knowledge that I am working for you, you do not rest. Inaction then would be the outcome of despair. My Hand is not shortened that it cannot save. Know that, repeat it, rely on it, welcome the knowledge, delight in it. Such a truth is as

a hope flung to a drowning man. Every repetition of it is one pull nearer shore and safety.[2]

You're Invited...

to Trust God Completely

WHAT:

An opportunity to settle in to God's love and faithfulness no matter what happens.

WHEN:

Each time your fear or worry causes you to question God's strength and promises. From this time onward, trust His plan for you. If you are in the middle of a hard time, know that God is in this situation with You. Trust Him to walk you through it whatever the outcome.

WHERE:

Wherever you are. Better yet, find a favorite nook in your bedroom, your school library, or in your backyard. Wherever you can be with the Lord without interruption is a good place to get on your knees and lift up all of your life to Him.

WHAT TO BRING:

The biggest trouble on your heart today. A loss. A fear. A change that calls you to courage. A friend's hurts. An argument you had with your parents. Whatever it is, bring it to God. Give it to Him and know He is bigger than this trouble. Rest in Him.

God Is Always Able

It's difficult to stay godly when things in life don't go as planned. We don't want inconvenience. We don't want to be tested. We're not even in the mood to be a witness to the participants in our unexpected drama. And when we miss an opportunity to say yes to God, there is something that happens within us: We doubt our faith and our original passion for Jesus.

Why do we tumble so far into doubt after even just once ignoring God's leading? The world goes on and God goes on, right? And our faith is way bigger than one moment of indifference. But we forget we have a great enemy to the peace we crave, one who loves to interrupt our lives at the most unsuspecting times. Satan wants to catch us off guard and use our reactions against us. He loves to whisper, "If you can't stay godly and obedient in the small mishaps of life, how do you think you're going to be able to pass the bigger tests and trials?" So, in the quietness of our hearts we ponder our reactions to life's situations. And if we find our attitude wanting, we label ourselves unable.

I don't qualify to be a girl who says yes to God. Look at how I acted: impatient, unkind, emotional, angry, unstable, and irrational.

We listen to the wrong voice. We choose Satan's naysaying or our own spiraling doubt and frustration. Next thing we know, we label ourselves, close up this book, and put it in the tall stack of other unfinished books that could nurture our faith.

I know because I did this for too long in my life. It wasn't until I settled God's amazing love in my heart that I finally understood what Lamentations 3:22-23 refers to when it tells us, "His compassions never fail. They are new every morning." Actually, God's compassions, or mercies, are available minute-by-minute, step-by-step, decision-by-decision, reaction-by-reaction. We don't have to get bogged down and label ourselves as unable. We just have to ask God for forgiveness and move on.

When you are tempted to tell yourself you cannot be a young woman of extraordinary faith, let your mind and heart rest in these words:

> *I am not to be labeled as unable. I am a child of God on a journey of learning how to make sure my reactions don't deny Christ's presence in me. I am a person who says yes to God not because my emotions and reactions are always perfect. No, I say yes to God because He is perfectly able to forgive me, love me, remind me, challenge me, and show me how to weather trials in ways that prove His Spirit resides in me. I remind myself often that people don't care to meet my Jesus until they meet the reality of Jesus in my life.*

As you study your Bible, you'll read and hear about Job. Some people don't like this book of the Bible. Or, let's say, they find it uncomfortable and they aren't sure what to do with it. But I love it because it's about what it looks like to face severe trouble and still be willing to trust God. Job lost everything and he rested in God.

Job was tested and challenged in ways most of us can't imagine. He experienced everything he ever feared: "If only my anguish could be weighed and all my misery be placed on the scales! It would surely outweigh the sand of the seas" (Job 6:2-3). Even Job's wife said to him, "Are you still maintaining your integrity? Curse God and die!" (Job 2:9). But Job had settled in his heart to trust God. "You are talking like a foolish woman," he told his wife. "Shall we accept good from God, and not trouble?" (Job 2:10). And because of that radical obedience, Job received a radical blessing in his relationship with the Lord. "My ears had heard of you but now my eyes have seen you" (Job 42:5). Job had known of God, but only through his trials and his obedience during those trials did he experience God personally. And why? Because he clung to his faith even when everyone and everything around him might suggest he was a fool to believe.

The psalmist David discovered this radical blessing—this intimate, deep relationship with God—when he settled in his heart to love God no matter what:

> My life is consumed by anguish and my years by groaning; my strength fails because of my affliction, and my bones grow weak...But I trust in you, LORD; I say, "You are my God." My times are in your hands; deliver me from the hands of my enemies, from those who pursue me. Let your face shine on your servant; save me in your unfailing love...How abundant are the good things that you have stored up for those who fear you, that you bestow in the sight of all, on those who take refuge in you...Praise be to the LORD, for he showed me the wonders of his love (Psalm 31:10,14-16,19,21).

With God's amazing love settled in our heart, we have His power to keep our faith steady and to experience lasting hope and joy independent of our situation.

It's true—God wants it all. All of us. All of our heart. All of our plans. And each and every moment of our lives. And it's in the exchange of what we want for what God wants that we experience the adventure and freedom and power of saying yes to God.

God is using all of your experiences, both good and bad, to develop your character to strengthen your ability to follow your calling.

After all, friend, you *never* know how God will use you until you let Him.

God's Word for You

Read Jeremiah 11:7-8. What does it mean to have a stubborn heart? When have you had a stubborn heart?

Read Proverbs 13:25 and write the word that describes the condition of the heart of those who live to make right choices that honor God.

Read 1 Peter 3:15 and record it here.

How are we to set apart Christ?

What does it mean for Him to be Lord?

Lord over what in our lives?

Read Psalm 84. Look at verses 1-2 and verse 10:

> How lovely is your dwelling place, LORD Almighty! My soul yearns, even faints, for the courts of the LORD; my heart and my flesh cry out for the living God...Better is one day in your courts than a thousand elsewhere; I would rather be a doorkeeper in the house of my God than dwell in the tents of the wicked.

This is a person who has decided to chase not after the world's emptiness, but rather God's fullness. The more you are satisfied with God, the more you crave to spend time with Him. This is how an extraordinary life of faith blossoms. In what area of life have you settled for the world's emptiness but are looking to change that by embracing God's fullness?

Read Psalm 84:4. What is a common characteristic for those abiding with the Lord?

Is it a common practice for you to praise the Lord? How could you incorporate more praise in your everyday relationship with God?

How does Psalm 84:9,11 encourage you?

What is in store for us when we say yes to God?

Living Y.E.S. (Your Extraordinary Story)

Have you ever spent time with God simply as another thing to check off your list of things to do?

What about this adventure of saying yes to God inspires you to view your time with God differently?

What are two ways you plan to make your time with Him more personal and more frequent?

1.

2.

List three examples of times when you have focused more on performance than on resting in God. Pray about them. Think about how different these events would have been if you had turned your attention to God and His leading.

1.

2.

3.

Comment on these statements from this chapter:

> I am not to be labeled as unable. I am a child of God on a journey of learning how to make sure my reactions don't deny Christ's presence in me. I am a person who says yes to God not because my emotions and reactions are always perfect. No, I say yes to God because He is perfectly able to forgive me, love me, remind me, challenge me, and show me how to weather trials in ways that prove His Spirit resides in me. I remind myself often that people don't care to meet my Jesus until they meet the reality of Jesus in my life.

When have you felt unable or unworthy?

What do you want to accomplish for God?

What else about this statement encourages you or challenges you?

Yes Prayer

Write a prayer asking God to make your time with Him more meaningful. Ask God to give you a deep desire for Him. The more time you spend with Him, the more you will crave being with Him. In Jesus' name, amen.

YES IN ACTION: SERVING OTHERS

A Note from Hope's Yes Journey

You've read about my family's amazing adventure adopting my two brothers more than ten years ago. That one *big* yes to God has led many more people to say yes to God in great ways.

I'm one of those people.

Even before my two brothers joined us at the family table, we knew they were a part of God's plan for us. My sisters and I had always wanted brothers. Prayed for brothers. Begged our parents for brothers. So when the decision was made to bring them home from Liberia, Africa, we were in awe the miracle was happening. Mom and Dad assured us it was real and God was behind it all—He tugged at their hearts, He prepared the boys and our family, and He called us all to say yes. Once we said yes as a family, I wanted to say yes to God in all areas of life.

That's when I promised God I'd be sold out to serving His people *everywhere*.

I went on my first mission trip four summers ago to Nicaragua, in Central America, and I fell in love with the whole experience. And I didn't fall in love because it was easy. Even though I had happily said yes, the trip was difficult. I was totally outside of my comfort zone. But any initial craziness and chaos gave way to great joy and peace.

After just a couple days it hit me: I was blessed by the people I came to help.

The following summer I went to Ethiopia, in Africa, for eight weeks. That was an incredible experience where I got to see a whole different way of life on the other side of the world. I was still experiencing the first jitters of being in a foreign land with a language, culture, and list of food preferences I didn't understand *at all*, but the adjustment time was shorter and my passion grew greater. Since that trip I have taken several more long trips to Nicaragua, including one just a few months ago where I helped run a foot-and-shoe clinic. We welcomed everyone who visited the clinic, and we'd wash their feet, pray for them, and then let them choose a pair of shoes from those we had been gathering for months before the trip. It was incredibly humbling.

The people of these two countries have been touched by God's grace. They are forever grateful for their lives. They have nothing of material value, yet their gratitude and joy flows without ceasing. They laugh, sing, dance, and give generously and without holding back...even to a stranger like me.

Mission trips have changed the way I look at the world and my life.

When I fully trust God with every decision, dream, and even doubt, a joy fills me and motivates me to be close to Him and to walk in His will. Whether my closet is full of cool clothes or my inbox is filled with e-vites shouldn't control my sense of value or joy. God's love is responsible for those.

My challenge to you is to ask God how He can use your life now and turn it into a mission field. You don't have to go overseas to do missions work. Look around you. Who has God placed right in front of you that needs help? Who in your family needs support? Which friend has been struggling with a temptation or a broken heart?

When God works through us to meet the needs of others— that's missions.

Turn your everyday life into God's mission field. You will be amazed at what He does when you step out of your comfort zone and partner with Him!

Hope

5

What Keeps Us from Saying Yes

Do you have a naysayer in your life? Someone who is negative about your passion to love God? Someone who says you are overly concerned about your purpose as a young woman of faith? I've had a few of these people in my life. It's difficult, isn't it? Even if we know some will not get our desire to please God, it is still painful when we're face-to-face with them. In your life, is it a friend, sibling, teacher, or stranger?

It's surprising when someone in our faith circles is our resident naysayer! That's what happened to me.

I could tell from her serious facial expression and stride that the woman approaching me had a few things on her mind. Sure enough, this woman in my Bible study thought I was taking my faith a little too seriously and God's Word a little too literally. After she dumped her load of concern on me, she smiled and encouraged me to lighten up. "Honey," she said, "I wouldn't want to see you carry this obedience thing too far."

How is that for a naysayer? If you choose the life of extraordinary faith, you are going to encounter such people. They don't understand you. They don't want to understand you. And often what you're doing makes them feel convicted. If someone is quick to find fault in something good someone else is doing, that person is usually wrapped up in his or her own self-centered outlook. Naysayers make themselves feel better by tearing others down. Paul warned Timothy about people like this:

> Mark this: There will be terrible times in the last days. People will be lovers of themselves, lovers of money, boastful, proud, abusive, disobedient to their parents, ungrateful, unholy, without love, unforgiving, slanderous, without self-control, brutal, not lovers of good, treacherous, rash, conceited, lovers of pleasure rather than lovers of God— having a form of godliness but denying its power. Have nothing to do with them (2 Timothy 3:1).

Your Yes Outshines Their No

Becoming a young woman who unashamedly says yes to God is going to cause you to be different from many of your family members and friends. You will examine life's circumstances with a different outlook. You will face life events with a different expectation. You will understand that just because life is busy doesn't mean you should bypass spending time with God. You understand your responsibility is to obey Him and He will handle the outcome. When you start to worry, you know how to get swept into God's assurance rather than swept away in fear. You will rely on a strength and power that simply does not make sense to most people.

While many naysayers may talk a good Christian game, they deny Christ in their attitudes and actions toward others. Instead of allowing those feelings of conviction to produce good changes in them, they seek to discourage you in hopes of hushing Christ in you.

It's not easy to keep their negativity from being discouraging, but as my husband always reminds me, "Lysa, consider the source." I ask myself, *Is this person who is criticizing me in active pursuit of a relationship with the Lord? Is this person answering God's call on his or her life, producing the evidence of Christ's fruit? Do they have my best interest at heart?* The answers are almost always no. So I look for any truth that might be in what this person has said, forgive him for any hurt he may have caused, and let the rest go.

What about when the person causing the hurt and becoming a source of discouragement is a strong believer? Even strong believers pursuing God can get pulled into ungodly attitudes. If only people had flashing signs above their heads that gave warning when they were operating in the flesh instead of the Spirit. Wouldn't that be great?

A wise friend once gave me a nugget of truth I think about often. She warned me as I stepped out and determined to say yes to God in all things, "Never let others' compliments go to your head or their criticisms go to your heart." Wow. That's incredible advice. We are so quick to absorb the criticisms that come our way. We will actually take those on as truth instead of trusting the truths we know about God and from God's Word that reveal to us our great value as His daughters.

In *The Purpose Driven Life,* author Rick Warren comments on naysayers:

> You will find that people who do not understand your shape for ministry will criticize you and try to get you to conform to what they think you should be doing. Ignore them. Paul often had to deal with critics who misunderstood and maligned his service. His response was always the same: Avoid comparisons, resist exaggerations, and seek only God's commendation.[1]

Rick then goes on to quote John Bunyan as saying, "If my life is fruitless, it doesn't matter who praises me, and if my life is fruitful, it doesn't matter who criticizes me."

That's so true!

The Enemies of Grace

Grace for the journey...we all need it. God is the only one we should be living for, and we need His grace to handle the successes and the failures, the applause and the criticism, and everything in-between. Sometimes our efforts will be fruitful and other times fruitless. But as long as we please God, it's all for good.

Grace has two fierce foes, though—acceptance and rejection. Imagine, for a moment, a huge stone wall with a guarded entrance. I approach it slowly. Puddles of mud dot the well-worn, barren ground. It is evident many have lingered here. Two gatekeepers wish to detain me. They wish to take my hand in friendship and have me remain on the outside of the wall. All the while, Jesus is standing on the other side of the wall in an open field full of beauty and adventure. So few people have made it past the gatekeepers into this field that the blades of grass remain unbroken and the flowers grow in abundance, unpicked and undisturbed.

The first gatekeeper is Acceptance. He requires much of me. He seems so enticing with his offerings of compliments and big promises, but though he is fun for a moment, soon my mind is flooded with concerns of being able to continue to impress him. I am quickly overwhelmed with pondering my interactions with others and keeping score on the table of comparison.

The second gatekeeper is Rejection. He also requires much of me. He seems appealing because he gives me permission to excuse myself from following my true calling. Yet he demands I pull back and shy away from the obedience for which my soul longs. His whispered questions of "What if?" and "What do they think of you?" linger in my mind and influence my actions and reactions.

How do I deny the lure of these two gatekeepers of grace? After all, I've tasted their laced fruit and, though I'm aware of their poison, I also crave their sweetness. If we look at the appeal of these two gatekeepers, we can see how they affect us daily.

Acceptance sings our praise. Rejection gives us lots of excuses.

Acceptance shines the limelight on and feeds the pride that is in our hearts.

Acceptance assures us that we, all on our own, are really something incredible and denies the reality that, but for the grace of Christ, we are empty.

Rejection presents us with a tempting look at how uncomplicated life could be if we settle for less. When you and I listen to him, we're likely to shrink back, pull inside ourselves, and give up or give in. Forget the wonders of an extraordinary faith because we have lost the desire to press on. The thought that we are really nothing eclipses the reality that, because of the grace of Christ in us, we *are* a treasured something.

So goes the battle in my heart. Honestly, it sickens me that I even give thought to and feel enticed by these life-draining agents of Satan. Jesus is standing behind these two slick gatekeepers. His arms are open, waiting to embrace and enfold me in the security of His truth. His truth is that I am precious and accepted, no matter what. No matter what choices I make, His love is not based on my performance. His love is based on His perfect surrender at the cross. But, I must choose to accept this love and walk this truth for it to make a difference in how I journey through life.

The Divide Between Desires

Pursuing obedience and saying yes to God has been the most

fulfilling adventure I have ever let my heart follow after. However, the journey has not been without bumps and bruises. I would be cheating you out of the whole truth in this chapter about what keeps us from radical obedience if I avoided discussing the divide between the desire of our flesh and the desire of God's Spirit in us. Our flesh seeks the approval of others, is swayed by Satan's voice of condemnation, and looks for the comfortable way out. God's Spirit in us opposes Satan and the world's way and offers an unexplainable peace that transcends the circumstances around us.

The divide can become narrow as I pay attention to the rather subtle voices in my head. If I'm not careful, I'll lose discernment and be unsure when a desire is of God or of my own flesh and humanness. Here's what you and I can pay attention to: the pull between condemnation and conviction. If I'm hearing thoughts of condemnation, these only come from Satan. There is no condemnation from Jesus, only conviction. It's important for us to know the difference. Condemnation leaves us feeling hopeless and worthless. Conviction invites us to make positive changes in our lives.

I also sometimes find myself getting caught up in my own weariness and grumbling over the empty places of life. These are the experiences that chip away at my contentment, that nag me into thinking I'm being cheated out of something somehow. Have you ever been unsatisfied with something that was actually a definite blessing? Think about the most recent incident of this in your life. Why do we do that to ourselves and risk setting back our faith journey progress?

I did this not that long ago. I was perfectly content and then I started to take a really picky look at life. Our recently renovated house was already starting to feel a bit smudged. With five kids and a dog, it didn't take long for the carpet to get stained and the woodwork to get scratched. My car has dings on each of the front doors and a scratch on the driver's side door, and sometimes this bothers me. We won't even talk about what the inside of my vehicle looks like! I even turned my pick-apart perspective on my family. I love my kids, but when they pout, complain, and whine… that bothers me. My husband and I are crazy about each other but still find ways to get on each other's nerves at times, and this bothers me. I struggle with trying to cram too much into too little time and often find myself running late—which really bothers me. When these little things get piled on top of bigger things, I can get discouraged.

This recent episode lasted several days. I became grumpy and dissatisfied in practically every area of life. Then there was a morning when I experienced that conviction from God. Believe me, I've had it many times so I recognized it when it was happening. It stirs in my heart and I feel discomfort about how I've been acting or thinking. I knew I had let unimportant problems become my source of contentment—or discontentment as the case turned out to be. I allowed my emotions to control my sense of joy.

When I feel the conviction of the heart, I know God has seen me and my heart in full view and He's telling me to take another look at what really matters. He isn't calling me an idiot for losing sight of His priorities. He's leading me back to His will and path for me. Jesus is our sweet, faithful Shepherd. I realize this more after each time He comes to find me when I get lost in the empty places—those thoughts, moods, and emotional places that are vast and scary. I try to fill them with worries about insignificant things, complaints about others, discontentment, and more self-loathing.

Do you ever get lost in the empty places?

Usually this happens to me when the busyness of life has crowded out my quiet times with Jesus. When I have not spent enough time allowing the Lord to refuel and refill me. When my soul feels heavy, these places can be distracting and difficult. And the reality is that sometimes we hurt and are discouraged. That's why conviction is so much different than condemnation. Condemnation would send me back into a hole where I would surely be crying over my wounds and feeling very alone and abandoned. God doesn't leave us as He reminds us what we are doing wrong. He remains with us so that we can continue on with greater strength in His grace.

Do You Worry or Worship?

When we find ourselves in these hard places, we do have God to help us find our way out of them, but we have to make choices. If we are slowly sinking in self-pity, anger, jealousy, or whatever else tops our list of ugly emotions, we must make the choice to either worry or worship. When we worry, we feel we have to come up with justifications and careful explanations for the naysayers (and sometimes we are our own naysayer). When we worry, we listen to the voices of Acceptance and Rejection. When we worry, we lie awake at night and ponder Satan's lies. When we worry, we have pity parties where the guests of honor are Negative Thinking, Doubt, and Resignation.

But we can make the choice to worship. When we worship in these hard places, we are reminded that none of this is about us— it's all about God. We turn our focus off of ourselves and back onto God Almighty. He can use empty places in your life to draw your heart to Him. He is the great love of your life who will never disappoint. He is building your eternal home that will never get broken, dirty, or need redecorating. He is preparing a place of eternal perfect fellowship where no one will be a naysayer. And heaven won't be limited to human time frames, so no one will ever be late...not even me!

Our hearts were made for perfection in the Garden of Eden, but the minute sin came into the picture, strokes of imperfection began to cloud everything. When we know Christ, however, we know this is not all there is. Realizing that this life is temporary helps me to live beyond this moment and rejoice in what is to come. Each time I feel my heart being pulled down into the pit of ungratefulness and grumbling, I recognize it as a call to draw near to the Lord. I thank Him for the empty places, for they remind me that only He has the ability to fill me completely. In my worship of Him, my soul is safe and comforted and reassured and at peace.

We all worship something. We must choose whom—or what—we will worship. Will it be the opinions of others, our fears, or even our own comfort? Or will it be the One who created our souls to worship? *Whatever we worship, we will obey.* As we choose to say yes to the Lord, we must be committed to choosing to worship Him and Him alone.

Peace like a River

What is the result of choosing to worship God, to obey Him alone? "Peace is the fruit of the obedient, righteous life."[2] If I am ever going to find peace past the naysayers, past the attacks of Satan, and past my own weariness, it will only be because I choose daily to walk in absolute obedience to the moment-by-moment, day-by-day, assignment-by-assignment commands of the Lord.

The prophet Isaiah writes, "If only you had paid attention to my commands, your peace would have been like a river, your well-being like the waves of the sea" (Isaiah 48:18). Did you catch the treasure hidden here? One of the most radical blessings for the woman saying yes to God is the peace that rushes through the soul of the one who is attentive to the Lord's commands.

God chose such a unique word to describe His peace—a river! A river is not calm and void of activity. It is active and cleansing and confident of the direction it is headed in. It doesn't get caught up with the rocks in its path. It flows over and around them, all the while smoothing their jagged edges and allowing them to add to its beauty rather than take away from it. A river is a wonderful thing to behold. Beth Moore says, "To have peace like a river is to have security and tranquility while meeting the many bumps and unexpected turns on life's journey. Peace is submission to a trust-worthy Authority, not resignation from activity."[3]

Jesus tells us His peace is unlike the world's peace: "Peace I leave with you; my peace I give you. I do not give to you as the world gives. Do not let your hearts be troubled and do not be afraid" (John 14:27). The world's way to peace would have me pull back to make life a little easier for my circumstances and my family. The problem with this is that we were not put here to be all about our-selves—we were put here to be all about God. We are to die to our self-centeredness so we can have more of Christ in our hearts and minds. Jesus clearly tells us to focus on Him, His ways, and His example, and His peace will be with us. The focus of our hearts and minds will shape our decisions and actions that follow: "You [God] will keep in perfect peace those whose minds are steadfast, because they trust in you" (Isaiah 26:3).

When we focus our mind and fix our attention on Christ, He is magnified and made bigger in our lives. When we focus our mind and fix our attention on life's obstacles, they will be wrongly magnified and made to appear larger than they really are. Our attention is like a magnifying glass—whatever we place it on becomes larger and more consuming of our time and energy. We desire to focus on Christ alone, but sometimes other things seem bigger, and so, without even realizing it, we shift our focus: "The flesh desires what is contrary to the Spirit, and the Spirit what is contrary to the flesh. They are in conflict with each other, so that you are not to do what you want" (Galatians 5:17). Before we know it, we are drawn into the muck and mire on the outer banks of Jesus' river of peace.

But sometimes it is down on your face in the mud in complete humility (and sometimes even humiliation!) that you will find a sweet and tender truth. It's from this position that you can say, "Jesus, I love You and want You more than anything else. I love You and want You more than the approval of my peers, family and friends, and even the naysayers in my life. I love You and want You more than the com-

Yes Factor

When you let the Messiah into the messy parts of your life, He can turn that experience into a great message of hope.

forts and trappings of this world. I love You and choose to believe Your truth over Satan's lies. I love You and choose to worship You and You alone. Jesus, I love You and want to come to You empty handed and offer my life in complete surrender."

Saying yes to God is a lot more about being than doing. It is choosing who I will worship and then depending on God to give me the strength to follow through. As my soul looks up from life's muck and rights the focus of its attention, I find myself pressing back into the river, where Jesus' peace rushes over me, refreshing, cleansing, and invigorating.

You're Invited...
to Focus on God

WHAT:

As you look around to find your next step, learn to keep your gaze on God and your heart fixed on His Word. God-focused living is the exciting key to your extraordinary adventure.

WHEN:

The next time you are worrying instead of worshipping. The next time you are panicking instead of praising. The next time you find yourself living in the empty place instead of following the Shepherd. These are the times you will want to look up at God and look only at Him. He'll show you the way back out.

WHERE:

Don't wait until you arrive at your church to turn your eyes to God. In fact, start this practice when you are in bed. When you first wake up and before your foot finds its way to your floor or to your pink, puffy slippers, say the prayer we learned in the first chapter. Do you remember it? Make this a daily call and commitment to saying yes to God.

God, I want to see You.
God, I want to hear You.
God, I want to know You.
God, I want to follow hard after You.
And even before I know what I will face today, I say yes to You.

This prayer centers your focus on God and leads your heart to communication with Him. After you say this prayer, keep talking to Him about your day ahead. This is the perfect time to rest in God and to give Him your whole day.

WHAT TO BRING:
Your eyes, your ears, your heart, and your biggest, most sincere YES!

A Little Girl's Dance

My touch has always comforted my youngest daughter, Brooke. I can remember running errands when she was a baby, knowing we should have been home an hour earlier for her nap. But also knowing there were things that had to get done, I pressed on, hoping for the best. She would start to get fussy, which made everyone else in the car start to lose patience. One of my older daughters, feeling very wise at five years old, said, "Mom, just tell her to stop crying. Tell her she'll get in big trouble if she doesn't."

Brooke wanted to get out of that car and she wanted to make sure we all knew it. What started as some whines and whimpers soon escalated into a full-blown meltdown complete with tears, wailing, and screaming.

I couldn't do much to comfort her while driving, but I could reach my arm into the backseat and gently pat her leg. It took a few minutes, but eventually she settled down and reached out her tiny hand to hold mine.

All of my kids like a hug, a pat on the shoulder, a hand of comfort on their back, but to Brooke these gentle touches seem to be a lifeline. Maybe touch is her love language. As Gary Chapman puts it in his book *The Five Love Languages,* touch might be the way Brooke will speak and understand love the most. Whatever it is, my touch is important to Brooke.

When Brooke was younger, she had a performance with her praise dance team from school. The girls looked especially beautiful that day dressed all in white, their hair pulled gently back from their faces, and each had an extra measure of grace in their step. I couldn't wait to see Brooke perform these dances she'd been working on and talking about for weeks. She loved getting up on a stage, so I expected her to be full of smiles and giggles. But just a few minutes before the performance was about to begin, a very distraught Brooke made her way to the audience to find me. With tears streaming down her cheeks, she explained that the teacher had moved her from the front row to the back row, and she didn't know the back row's part. I assured her everything would be fine. I whispered, "Honey, just get up there and watch the other girls for cues and follow in step. You know this dance, Brooke. You'll be fine."

She sobbed back, "I won't be fine if I mess up, and I know I'm going to mess up."

That's when it occurred to me. She would need my touch to get through this. But she and I both knew that it would not be possible for my arm to reach all the way up to the stage. So I quickly whispered, "Brooke, lock your eyes with mine, and Mommy will touch you with my smile. Don't look at anyone or anything else. Don't even look at the other girls dancing. It doesn't matter if you mess up. What matters is that you keep your eyes on me the whole time. We'll do this together."

Quietly she asked, "The whole time, Mommy?"

"The whole time, Brooke," I replied as I watched my brave girl walk away to take her place in line.

Several times during the dance, Brooke fell out of step. Her arms would go down when the rest of the back row lifted theirs up. She would go left and bump into the others headed right. She knew her steps weren't perfect, so her eyes brimmed with tears.

However, the tears never fell. With her eyes perfectly locked on my smiling face, she danced. She danced when the steps came easy. She danced when her steps got jumbled. She danced even when her emotions begged her to quit. She danced the whole way through. She danced and I smiled.

I smiled when her steps were right on track. I smiled when they weren't. My smile was not based on her performance. My smile was born out of an incredible love for this precious, courageous little girl. As she kept her attention focused solely on my smile and the touch of my gaze, it was as if the world slowly faded away and we were the only ones in the room.

This is the way God wants you and me to dance through life.

Though we can't physically see Him, our souls can picture Him so clearly. In our mind's eye He is there. The touch of His gaze wraps about us, comforts us, assures us, and makes the world's troubles seem distant and small. As long as our gaze is locked on His, we dance and He smiles. The snickers and jeers of others fade away. Even our missteps don't cause feelings of defeat. Our steps can so often betray the desires of our hearts, but it isn't our perfect performances that capture His attention. Instead, it is our complete dependence on Him and His never-distracted gaze.

He then whispers, "Hold on to Me and what I say about you. For My words are the truth of who you are and the essence of what you were created to be." I then imagine Him pausing and, with tears in His eyes and a crack in His voice, He adds, "Then you will know the truth, and the truth will set you free" (John 8:32).

His truth frees you from the chains of doubt and despair. His truth frees you from feeling unable and inadequate to try and pursue God in an all-out way. His truth washes over you and frees you to whisper, "I want to be a young woman who says yes to God." And in that moment, with your eyes locked on His, you are.

God's Word for You

When faced with the choice to worry or to worship, Scripture will be a powerful reminder of God's certain help.

Read Matthew 6:26-27. What good will worry do?

Read Matthew 6:30-32. What does God promise for our provision?

Read Mark 13:10-11. While you probably won't be arrested for preaching the gospel, you may find yourself in a situation where you are worried how to speak. How does this comfort you?

Instead of worrying, the mark of our lives should be worship. Worship replaces anxiety brought on by fear with an unexplained peace that can only come from focusing on God. "My *eyes* are *fixed* on you, Sovereign Lord; in you I take refuge—do not give me over to death" (Psalm 141:8, emphasis added). What worry do you need God's peace to cover right now?

Remember the story I shared about Brooke fixing her eyes on me? What does "fixed" in Psalm 141:8 mean? What does taking refuge in the Lord mean? How can we fix our eyes on the Lord?

Read Isaiah 30:21. What voice is being referred to here?

What direction will this voice give us?

How does this calm your worries?

[Let us fix] our eyes on Jesus, the *author* and *perfecter* of faith, who for the joy set before Him endured the cross, despising the shame, and has sat down at the right hand of the throne of God (Hebrews 12:2 NASB, emphasis added).

What does it mean that Jesus is the author of our faith?

What does it mean that Jesus is the perfecter of our faith?

How does this verse comfort and encourage you?

Living Y.E.S. (Your Extraordinary Story)

One way you and I can become God-focused is by learning God's Word and His promises for us. We've explored some powerful verses in this chapter and in the Bible study portion. Below, write out word-for-word two verses you want to spend time learning, knowing, and memorizing. Below each verse, write out why that message turns your eyes and heart toward Jesus and is important for you right now.

Verse 1:

Verse 2:

Most of us are only willing to trade in our worry and panic when we understand there is something different, something better for us. God blesses us with righteous alternatives to our human concerns and needs. It's time to trade up. It's time to exchange your empty places for God's abundance, hope, healing, and satisfaction.

In the spaces below, list the reasons you have to praise God and the reasons you are drawn to worship Him. What about His character compels you to call out to Him, sing praises, lift up prayers, and truly worship Him as Lord and Savior? When we let go of the stresses of this world and trade up to God's big picture and purpose, it changes our hearts forever.

I will stop panicking about _____

Instead, I will praise God for _____

I will stop panicking about _____

Instead, I will praise God for _____

I will stop worrying about _____

Instead, I will worship God because _____

I will stop worrying about _____

Instead, I will worship God because _____

Yes Prayer

Saint Patrick was kidnapped as a teen from his native land of Britain and forced to be a slave for six years in Ireland. During his captivity, his job was tending sheep. He spent many hours each day in prayer. By the time he escaped back to Britain, he had become a man sold out for the cause of Christ. Several years later, he returned as a missionary to Ireland and lived out his life winning that country to Christ.

His circumstances often could have caused a lot of worry. Instead, he made the choice to worship God and trust His plan. The following was his constant prayer. I hope you will be comforted and encouraged by it.

Christ shield me this day:
Christ with me,
Christ before me,
Christ behind me,
Christ in me,
Christ beneath me,
Christ above me,
Christ on my right,
Christ on my left,
Christ when I lie down,
Christ when I arise,
Christ in the heart of every person who thinks of me,
Christ in every eye that sees me,
Christ in the ear that hears me.

SAINT PATRICK,
FROM HIS BREASTPLATE

God, when I start to focus back on the world or on my list of worries, remind me to keep my eyes locked on You. You will not look away. You see me and know me, and You know the amazing purposes I was born for. If I take a step in the wrong direction, You do not look away. When others let me down, You are still right here beside me. You are my Shield and my Shepherd. I am so grateful. In Jesus' name, amen.

6

Yes Is About Delight

I was discouraged.

My life was wonderfully fulfilling and clicking right along and then…you know how it goes. All of a sudden I was standing in the middle of the wreckage that was my life. I was surrounded by mini disasters and major emotions. My computer went on the blink and some very important documents disappeared. A big book deal I was excited about fell through. Our well broke, and we had to go several days without water. A diamond fell out of my wedding ring.

Then at the top of this heap of haphazard happenings was a big setback. My husband blew out his knee and had to have major reconstructive surgery, leaving him bedridden for nearly five weeks.

I didn't know whether to laugh or cry. A friend of mine hit the nail on the head when she said, "Lysa, I think when you go with God to a new level, you get a new devil." While I'm not sure about the exact theological correctness of that statement, I do know Satan hates the extraordinary faithful soul who says yes. He hates it when a person jumps off the fence of complacency into the center of God's will. There's a spiritual battle raging around us and, because of that, life can be hard.

While saying yes to God does bring blessing, it's not easy. If our desire for obedience is born merely out of duty, we may be quick to give up. However, if our desire is born out of delight, out of a love relationship that burns deep in our soul, it won't be extinguished— no matter the cost.

Are you facing a deeper relationship with God *and* a "new devil"? Let's explore how the latest inconveniences and discomforts in your life are an important part of your yes journey. In fact, they are probably stretching, strengthening, and growing your faith in ways you haven't even realized yet.

Purpose, Perspective, and Persistence

I don't know about you—but I love a great love story! And one of my favorite love stories is from the Bible. It is the enduring, persevering romance between Jacob and Rachel. Jacob's love for Rachel gave him purpose and perspective, which led to amazing persistence. He served Rachel's father for many years to earn the right to marry her because he loved her that much: "Jacob served seven years to get Rachel, but they seemed like only a few days to him because of his love for her" (Genesis 29:20).

Do you see what love can do for a person's view of his circumstances? When you are crazy in love with someone, you'll do anything for him—and do it with the highest level of sheer joy. I want to be so crazy in love with Jesus that not only do I serve Him, but I do it with absolute delight.

A real sign of a young woman on the yes journey is that she looks to God not for comfort and convenience but for purpose and perspective—like Jacob did. Comfort and convenience lead to complacency. When trouble comes, the complacent person becomes critical of everyone, including God. Have you ever been around someone who didn't want to try at a sport or a hard class at school? They tend to become the complainers about those pursuits, quick to find fault with the activity or to pick apart the people who are trying.

On the other hand, purpose and perspective lead to the perseverance that is evident in those living a devoted life. The persistent person eagerly looks to handle trials and struggles in a way that honors God and allows personal growth. What challenge is in your path right now? If you view it as a chance to give God glory and to draw closer to His purpose for you, how does that change things?

Because we love God, we look for and trust in His purpose in everything. The persistent person understands the meaning of Romans 8:28: "We know that in all things God works for the good of those who love him, who have been called according to his purpose." This does not mean that everything that happens to us will be good, but that God will work in and through every situation to bring good from it. And let's not miss the last four words of this verse, where we are reminded that it is all "according to his purpose." God has a purpose, and His plans to accomplish that purpose are perfect. Trusting His good purpose, and seeking to understand that He takes all the events from our life and orchestrates good from them, leads to a changed perspective.

Seeing God in Everything

Our changed perspective helps us see God in everything. I am convinced that Satan wants to keep my perspective in a place where my heart is discouraged and my mind is questioning God. Yet the Bible calls me to a different action: "We also glory in our sufferings, because we know that suffering produces perseverance; perseverance, character; and character, hope" (Romans 5:3-4). God's Word calls me to rejoice! Not that I rejoice in the bad things—I would have to fake that. But I *can* rejoice in what God is doing in me through difficult times.

When Art hurt his knee, we prayed this would be a minor injury and surgery wouldn't be required. We just knew God was going to go before us and make the way smooth. However, when the test results came back, we were facing a worst-case scenario. Not only would Art have to have surgery, but it was one of the worst knee injuries the doctor had ever seen. Simply looking at the circumstances and the doctor's report, we might have been tempted to get pulled into Satan's lies that God had not answered our prayers, that He wasn't trustworthy. However, the truth is that God is faithful and true, and His Word promises us, "He has not despised or scorned the suffering of the afflicted one; he has not hidden his face from him but listened to his cry for help" (Psalm 22:24).

So what do we do with the fact that my very athletic husband is out of commission for several months? What does he do about missing weeks of work and having his life totally interrupted? What do I do with my feelings of being overwhelmed and frustrated because I need his help with the kids? What do I do with the fact that he can't drive, is in extreme pain, and needs my unconditional love and support—even on the days when I'm too tired to give it?

Okay, God. Where are You? I cried out. There were too many details and too much stress. Honestly, I started to get a little frustrated with God. Satan was having a field day.

Provision, Protection, and Process

What do you do when you feel as though God isn't hearing your cries for help? Or, worse yet, He's saying no?

It hasn't been easy, and God has had to remind me several times, but here's what I do know: God *always* hears me when I cry out to Him, and when He says no, it's for my provision, my protection, and it's part of the process of growing me more like Christ.

Provision

On one of my "Woe is me, my husband is still in bed and I am doing everything" days, I took my kids along with a friend's child out to lunch. I was determined to have a good attitude, but with each whiney response and sibling spat I could feel my blood pressure rising. I was at the counter trying to place my order and keep an eye on the kids sitting in the booth across the restaurant when a lady came up and put her hand gently on my shoulder. "I've got your napkins and straws," she said, "and I'll put them on your table." I was shocked. Who was this sweet stranger?

After I made my way back to my table, I found her sitting with her family and went over to thank her. When I did, she told me that when I walked into the restaurant, God told her to help me. She didn't know who I was until I turned around to talk to her at the counter, and she recognized me as the speaker from a women's conference she attended last spring. She then went on to ask me if she could make my family a meal. I told her my husband had just had surgery and a meal would be great.

I walked back to my booth with tears in my eyes. Just that morning I had cried out to God to fill in the gaps where I was feeling weary and weak. I asked Him to be my portion of all I needed to take care of my family that day. God was answering my prayer! My perspective totally changed. God was working good through Art's surgery and our needs. He didn't stop the surgery, and He also didn't leave us in that hard spot. He was teaching us about His provision.

How can He be our Ultimate Provider if we aren't ever in need? I was so touched by this lady's obedience to God's call to reach out to me. I was blown away by the personal and practical way He answered my cries for help despite my bad attitude.

Do you see how cool this is? God takes care of us in many ways, including through the obedience and faith of others. Sometimes you will be the one responding and doing something for another. You may realize right away why that action helped someone or you may walk away never knowing if it helped or served them. You *will* know, however, that you followed God with a big yes that day.

Other times you will be the one receiving that word of encouragement or an offer of help with a class project or how to program your new phone. Maybe someone will invite you to talk about your heart and your worries and ask to pray for you. Those sweet moments are when we feel God's great provision in amazing, everyday ways.

Protection

My husband is an avid runner and can often be seen running the country roads near our home. After his knee injury, he was very disappointed, to say the least, when the doctor told him it could be up to a year before he could run again—and that some people with this type of injury have to give up running altogether. Anytime we have to take a break from something we really enjoy, it's hard. But the thought of forever giving up running seemed too much to swallow.

Then came the call from a friend who knew of a man who was injured playing flag football the same week that Art had been injured, only the doctors were telling him he would never walk again. He was now paralyzed from the waist down. Then another call came from a friend who told me she read in the paper of a man riding his bike on the same roads my husband runs on. This man was struck by a car and killed.

Art and I had been so quick to throw a pity party over our circumstances, but now we realized God had protected him from situations that could have been a lot worse.

I confess I don't always understand the ways of God in these circumstances—why Art would just need surgery while another man lay paralyzed and another man was killed. Many have had to go through severe circumstances and unfathomable pain, and my own family is no exception. We have experienced tragedy, but I know that I know that I know this: God has worked good in every one of these situations. As I look back and reflect on our difficult times, I can see how He has protected us.

Process

Ultimately, our time here on earth is for one single purpose: to grow more and more like Christ. Each of us comes to a place in our Christian journey where we have to make the decision whether we will become part of that process or not. I wrote a poem to express that moment of decision:

> *A man journeyed to a place*
> *Where the road caused him to ponder,*
> *Should he travel the wide, clear road?*
> *Or should he venture up the other?*
>
> *The wide road was more often traveled,*
> *It was level and easy and clear.*
> *The narrow one seemed barely a path,*
> *With very few footprints there.*
>
> *His senses said to choose for ease*
> *And walk where many have wandered.*
> *But the map he held in his hand*
> *Showed the narrow going somewhere grander.*
>
> *In life we will all come to a point*
> *Where a decision must be made.*

Will we choose to walk with comfort's guide?
Or journey the narrow path God says?

We want to live the totally sold-out life for Christ, yet there are other things pulling at us, enticing us, calling out to us—causing our indecision. Brent Curtis and John Eldredge said it well in their book *The Sacred Romance*:

> At some point on our Christian journey, we all stand at the edge of those geographies where our heart has been satisfied by less-wild lovers, whether they be those of competence and order or those of indulgence. If we listen to our heart again, perhaps for the first time in a while, it tells us how weary it is of the familiar and indulgent. We find ourselves once again at the intersection with the road that is the way of the heart. We look down it once more and see what appears to be a looming abyss between the lovers we have known and the mysterious call of Christ.[1]

In times where the road diverges in front of us, we can either fall away from God or fall toward Him. During Art's long healing process, he made the decision to fall toward God and humbly thank Him for allowing the injury to happen. He chose to look for opportunities every day to rejoice in this trial and make the most of being still and quiet. He dove into God's Word and spent hours praying, reading, and writing notes about all God was teaching him.

Christmas happened to fall right in the middle of Art's recovery. Every Christmas morning we have a special breakfast with Jesus where we give Him a gift from our heart. I wondered what gift Art would have this year. When his turn came, he said he wanted to look for a way to serve another or give to another in Christ's name every day for the next year. By next Christmas he would know that 365 people's lives were made better because of Christ in him. Throughout the following months our dinnertime conversations each night centered around what "God adventures" Daddy had participated in that day. Soon, we were all sharing our own ways that we listened to God. My sweet husband made a choice to rejoice in the process of growing more like Christ, and what a difference it made not only in his life, but in others' lives as well.

My kids do this and really get into it. What I know about being a young woman trying to figure out life and faith is that it is so important and wonderful to talk about your faith and make going to church a priority. Talking to friends and your family about your adventures with God reinforces God's message and purpose for you. More times than not, when I'm feeling like having a pity party, I will speak to another friend of faith, and as soon as I hear about what God is doing in her life, I'm inspired, excited, and eager to take another look at my situation. Often, I have stopped seeing what God is doing in my own life!

So when my family shares what heart gift they want to give to Jesus, I have great joy and hope. I see how they are willing to reach out to others, take risks as Christians, and how they are also learning to discern when a decision is right in God's eyes. This is one of the most special family traditions we have. It is so dear to me and to each member of our family.

I'll confess that there are some Christmases when I wish deeply that I had experienced this kind of relationship with my earthly father. I wish he had sat with me and asked about what God was doing in my life and how I was living out my faith. This brings tears to my eyes to think about. But I didn't have that in my earthly father. And maybe you don't either. Or maybe your family gets so busy that they forget about pausing to talk about God and be with God as a family. Here's what I want you to know...your heavenly

Father wants to be with you just like this. Talk to Him. Share with Him. The delight I have when my kids share about their growth is just a teeny tiny spark compared the brilliant explosion of joy God has when we talk to Him. And do you know what? Maybe your faithfulness in this way will start a new tradition for your family. Maybe this will be the gift you give Jesus this year or next year… the year you invite your family to spend more time with Him.

What happens when we start sharing about the good of the Lord manifesting in our lives? Everything changes, that's what! My husband's injury and time spent recovering turned out to be a blessing. What we gained as a family during this time was more than a new perspective; it was a gift from God. This time of looking for ways to serve God like never before prepared our hearts for the night we met our boys in August of that year. We were all so in tune with saying yes to God in the little things that when this big thing came, we faced it head-on. We didn't run away with a trail of good excuses flying about behind us like dust on a dirt road. No, we looked at the opportunity before us, asked for God's will to be done, and leaped into the unknown with nothing but God's sweet confirmations.

Yes Factor

Ask God to let you see every person, decision, circumstance, hurt, hope, and possibility through His eyes.

Look at all that might have been missed had God answered our prayers about Art's knee the way we *wanted* Him to. We wanted a quick, easy healing where life could carry on. God wanted life interrupted. God wanted our attention. God wanted to give a huge blessing wrapped in a most unlikely package.

Let's revisit the great wisdom of the prophet Jeremiah: "Because of the LORD's great love we are not consumed, for his compassions never fail. They are new every morning; great is your faithfulness. I say to myself, 'The LORD is my portion; therefore I will wait for him'" (Lamentations 3:22-24). God is our portion of protection and peace. He's our portion of provision and security. He's our portion of all of the joy and patience we need during the process of growing more like Christ. He is our portion of whatever we need, whenever we need it—if only we'll recall His goodness and ask Him.

We have Jesus and His power, and that power is able to completely change our outlook on life. This is how we can find the kind of joy the apostle Peter talks about: "Though you have not seen him, you love him; and even though you do not see him now, you believe in him and are filled with an inexpressible and glorious joy" (1 Peter 1:8). The ability to have a radically different perspective is the extraordinary blessing of those who choose an extraordinary faith.

We're human. We know we're not always going to like our circumstances. Just because I am a woman who says yes to God does not mean I always like the things that come my way on any given day. I don't wake up every morning and think, *Joy, joy, joy. Another day of more challenges or reasons to get moody and tired and worn out.* No, I wake up and say, "God, I love You and choose to accept the assignments You place before me with an attitude that reflects the truth that You live in me. I know I won't do this perfectly, and I admit my inability to do this in my strength. So, I say yes to You today. I say yes to Your desire to invade my natural flesh responses. I say yes to Your forgiveness when I mess up. I say yes to persevering even when I want to give up. I say yes to Your invitation to be obedient even when other paths seem more appealing. I say yes even as my lips desire to utter a thousand times over, 'I can't.' I say yes to loving You more."

You're Invited...
to Trade Duty for Delight!

WHAT:

It is a resale store for your old perspectives! Trade in those outdated, limited, ordinary blah-faith words and ideas and exchange them for the extraordinary-faith words and perspectives of yes. It's the best deal of your life! No more drudgery. This is about delight.

WHEN:

The sooner you learn the language of yes, the better equipped you will be for the yes journey. Grace. Abundance. Hope. Faith. Divine appointments. Joy. Peace. Miracles. Forgiveness. Acceptance. Unconditional love. Possibilities. Isn't this a great vocabulary?

WHERE:

Your room, your kitchen table, or maybe in a circle of friends who are ready for the yes journey. Choose a place where you can all speak openly and hang out long enough for everyone to share.

WHAT TO BRING:

Your Bible, your journal or a notepad, and a favorite pen. Gather every word you use that is tied to "duty" and write a list. These are the words you will exchange for words of delight. For example, "Have to," "Can't." and "That's too hard"...those are phrases tied to duty and not to faith. Write beside them words you've learned in our journey together and in the Bible that express possibility. For example, "I get to," "God can through me," and "Opportunity."

No More "I Can'ts"

Two little words have become such a part of our mental dialogue: "I can't." And there are times they reflect a bit of truth. Hey, I can't fly through the air like Superman. I can't make my scalp suddenly start growing the silky straight blond hair like the Pantene hair model. I can't grow a tree in my backyard that sprouts dollar bills. These statements are truths born from cold hard facts and not from my own laziness or fear.

But other "I can't" statements *are* often born from laziness or fear. Assumptions that have been around so long that they feel like truth. Last summer I decided to take an honest assessment of some of these "I can't" statements in my life. As I marched up to each of these giants, I asked myself the question: *What would it take to slay this giant in my life?* Most of the time, the answer was as simple as a decision: *Decide that I ought to, I can, and I will.*

I shared this sentiment with a friend who was struggling with her own "I can't." She knew God was calling her to be a speaker and a writer and had signed up for a conference our ministry offers every year called She Speaks. Then the doubts and fears started to overwhelm her. A letter she sent to me was full of those doubts and I could tell she was second-guessing that she heard God right and that she was capable of going to the conference and following God's lead. So, to encourage her, I started an email to her that read:

> I love your honesty, sweet friend. I also love your heart. Though you are scared, you are walking that narrow road of absolute obedience. God is pleased.
>
> Now to address your questions and fears. First of all, you are not an idiot at all. You have taken a step toward a dream God has placed in your heart. That makes you obedient, not idiotic. I am so proud of you for doing more

than 90 percent of all people who lurk in the shadows of their dreams but never get intentional about them…

Wait a minute.

Before I could continue I felt the gentle nudging in my heart I've come to recognize as God's voice. He brought to my mind another conversation I'd had with this friend where she'd shared about running several times a week with a group of ladies from her neighborhood. She was getting in such good shape and feeling great. I had just smiled and nodded while thinking, *I could never run that far or be that disciplined.*

God brought this past conversation to my mind, I'm convinced, to challenge me. How could I ask her to step out of her comfort zone into a world where I feel comfortable, that of speaking and writing, if I wasn't willing to do the same? My advice and encouragement would mean so much more to her if I stepped into her comfort zone and pushed through my own fears. It was time to strap on my tennis shoes and run.

Running more than a mile or two was a big "I can't" in my life, but I felt God telling me to go out and run until I couldn't run anymore. Every time my body wanted to stop, I was to pray for my friend. I ran and ran and ran. When I finally stopped, I immediately got in my car and clocked how far I'd gone. I was shocked as the odometer turned to a little more than three miles. I had done it. I threw my hands up in victory and prepared to retire my tennis shoes for eternity.

That is, until a few days later when God nudged my heart again to run. I continued to run several times a week over the next month and prayed for my friend every time my side ached, my breathing became labored, and my legs cried out for me to stop. I pushed through the "I can't." Then, the day before the conference I threw my hands up as I victoriously exclaimed, "I can!" That day I clocked 8.6 miles.

My friend was also victorious that weekend at the conference we both attended. She didn't back down or back out. She was absolutely delighted. And you'd better believe that we carved out time early one morning during the conference to run together. In both of our situations there was nothing standing in our way but our own minds, and our minds were ready to focus on what we could do with God and in His strength.

What You Can Do

I was at a conference in California when my daughter Ashley called me on my cell phone. I could tell she was tearing up as she said, "Mom, I need you to pray for me." I stepped outside to give her my full attention. I assured her I would pray for her throughout the weekend and that I also wanted to pray with her right that minute. I asked what was troubling her. Her answer stunned me.

She was asking for me to pray that she would have the strength to continue a fast she'd started that morning. Two little boys from her school had recently lost their dad to cancer. She told me God had clearly spoken to her heart that morning and challenged her to pray and fast for that family all day. She did exactly what He had told her to do, but now her stomach was really hurting and she was having a hard time.

I checked my watch and calculated that it would be around 9:00 p.m. East Coast time. I encouraged her that sometimes God just intends a fast to be from sunup to sundown and I was sure He'd be fine with her eating a little something before going to bed. She replied back, "Mom, I know exactly what God told me to do and I want to be obedient. I did not call for you to talk me out of this. I just need for you to pray for me to have the strength to continue."

Ashley got it! She wasn't saying "I can't." She knew that in God's strength she could do this. She didn't want an out. She just wanted help to stick to her "I can."

By the time I walked back into that speaking engagement, I looked like a wreck. My hair was windblown and my makeup tear streaked, but my soul was overflowing with the joyful knowledge that my precious daughter was becoming a true disciple, a young woman who says yes to God! I knew that in the morning, after her day of faithfulness and obedience, she would experience a deep, genuine delight in the Lord.

I can assure you that on the other side of every "I can't" excuse is a glorious adventure with God just waiting to happen. And rest assured, the victory is not found in your performance. Rather, it's in your pursuit of taking that first step with God. A joy will be there like you've never known. As we choose to say "With God, I can," we can expect Him to show up and be our daily portion of everything we need. Don't be afraid of the outcome; that's in God's hands. You just rest in the delight that walking with God this way is what your soul was designed for. The more you experience Him, the more you expect to see and hear from Him every day. Obedience stops being a dutiful obligation and starts becoming a delight you crave.

When a young woman says yes to God, she discovers an exceptional, extraordinary way to live.

God's Word for You

Write your thoughts on this statement:

> If our desire for obedience is born merely out of duty, we may be quick to give up. However, if our desire is born out of delight, out of a love relationship that burns deep in our soul, it won't be extinguished—no matter the cost.

What does serving God out of duty look like?

What does serving God out of delight look like?

Psalm 37:3-4 says,

> "Trust in the Lord and do good; dwell in the land and enjoy safe pasture. Take delight in the Lord, and he will give you the desires of your heart."

Where will we find safety?

What will you be given as a result of delighting in the Lord?

How will the desires of our heart change as a result of having a love relationship with God?

What are some of the "I can'ts" in your life right now?

Second Corinthians 12:8-10 says,

> "Three times I pleaded with the Lord to take it away from me. But he said to me, 'My grace is sufficient for you, for my power is made perfect in weakness.' Therefore I will boast all the more gladly about my weaknesses, so that Christ's power may rest on me. That is why, for Christ's sake, I delight in weaknesses, in insults, in hardships, in persecutions, in difficulties. For when I am weak, then I am strong."

Do these verses give you an excuse to remain weak and to stick to your "I can't"? Or do they tell you where you can draw strength from?

How do we tap into the strength of the Lord and use it to help us?

Living Y.E.S. (Your Extraordinary Story)

Saying yes to God isn't about comfort and convenience but is about purpose and perspective. How have you, in the past, tried to make faith about comfort instead of purpose?

Describe a time when you chose not to follow God's leading because it was inconvenient. Now, with a renewed perspective, why would you be motivated to say yes in a similar situation?

What excites you about the idea of God working in you and through others to provide for everyone?

How is God leading you to be part of His provision plan for someone else?

How has God helped you recently by leading someone else to support, encourage, or assist you in some way?

Think about a tough situation you've faced recently. Describe this experience and how there was evidence of God's:

Provision:

Protection:

Process:

What assignments has God been giving to you lately? How are they challenging you?

Yes Prayer

God, I love having my eyes open to all that You do and all that You are in my life and in the lives of others. I'm excited to start seeing the times when my friends and I are faithful in following Your will and Your leadings. I am taking a vow today to be more present and more available. Keep me from resisting Your leading with a bunch of "I can't" statements. How will I ever know Your great power and grace unless I take a leap of faith?

Help me, Lord. I want to experience the shift from duty to delight as I honor You in all that I do. Today I pray specifically for Your provision and protection in the following areas:

And I pray for Your provision and protection for my friend
_____ in these specific ways:

God, may Your wise and awesome will be done in our lives.
In Jesus' name, amen.

YES IN ACTION: REACHING OUT
A Note from Hope's Yes Journey

Sometimes when God speaks to me I am a little reluctant to actually do what it is He has called me to do. But one particular incident showed me how our obedience matters. On a winter night I was driving down a back road near my house. It was dark and nothing was visible without the car's headlights beaming onto it.

Up ahead, I could barely make out a black blob on the side of the road. As my car approached, I realized it was a person. I was going too fast to stop right there, and, honestly, it didn't occur to me to stop and see who it was. But as I passed and the distance between me and the figure became greater in the rearview mirror, God's voice was calling me. I knew I was supposed to turn around and see who it was. God was asking me to pay attention and not shrug off His leading. I turned the car around to get another look.

As I got closer to the figure, I saw a girl with long blond hair. She looked about my age, maybe younger. I realized I had seen her once before. It was then that I felt it was safe to slow down beside this girl. God was asking me to not only pay attention, but to reach out.

When I pulled up beside the girl, I saw tears running down her cheeks. As she saw me motion for her to get in the warmth of the car, a look of gratefulness and relief covered her face. I didn't ask any questions. Her pain seemed too deep for her to share. I took her to her destination and told her God loved her and that I was there for her anytime. As she got out of the car, I handed her a napkin with my number on it and that was it.

I didn't expect anything to come out of this encounter with

the blond girl. Little did I know God had great plans for this girl and I had a huge part in them.

Months later she contacted me and asked if we could go get lunch. That was the beginning of a long friendship between us. I started bringing her to church and introducing her to friends. God was definitely at work in her life. Before long, the girl accepted Christ. When she was given the opportunity to share her testimony, she asked me to come and support her while she shared her story to a hundred other teens. As the details of that dark night unfolded, I realized exactly why God asked me to pick her up.

She was on her way to end her life.

She had a rough time of things in her home, and that night she had gotten into a huge fight with her parents and walked out. She felt alone and desperate. If I hadn't turned around my car and picked her up, she might not be alive today.

God isn't asking us to pick up strangers from the side of the road, but He is asking us to notice those requests for obedience. Had I determined it wasn't safe to stop, I still would've had a way to respond to God's leading by praying for the person. When we sense that someone needs the Lord, we can pray for them and their needs, whatever those needs might be. God knows.

Can you imagine what opportunities and possibilities would unfold if we paid attention to God's voice and started living sold-out to His calling on a daily basis?

I'm so thankful I let go of my pride, fear, or any other road-blocks I could've put between me and God's leading. Instead, that night I followed God's lead. As a result, I was part of His amazing plan to show love and purpose to a special girl.

Hope

7

Giving Up What Was Never Ours

Do you remember Hope's confession in the first Yes in Action entry? That story about my daughter when she was nine makes me want to laugh and cry at the same time. How much she has grown in her yes journey since then! That gives me great delight. But the other side of the emotion coin is a sense of guilt about my own meltdowns. No matter how much we grow, there will be times when we act just like Hope did, holding on tightly to something that really isn't ours to begin with. Whatever it is you hold on to, it belongs to God. It's God's money. It's God's plan. It's God's relationship. It's God's gift of a talent to us. Yes, even your talents are God's to be used for His amazing purposes.

If you're one of those fortunate young women who can sing, your voice and ability belong to God. And just as I knew something better was waiting for Hope if she was willing to let go of that bill, *God knows* that something better is waiting for us when we willingly let go of our abilities, ideas, dreams, financial blessings, and belongings.

God has special knowledge about our lives. Do you give that reality enough power when you are praying to Him? He knows all. He knows what has happened and what will happen. He knows how we can honor Him. He knows which paths will cause us to stumble. Have you ever been mad at God because you wanted so badly to know everything He does? Well, He isn't keeping secrets from us. We have open communication with Him and His leading is true and real, but we have to *ask* for it, *listen* to it, and *act in* it when the time comes. That means "Let go of that ten-dollar bill!"

The blessings that follow our faithful yes are great. The question is, do we trust Him? Do we trust He will bless us? Do we trust His blessings are infinitely better than what He might first ask us to release?

The Unlimited Blessing Plan

Trust. Isn't that why more of us don't offer all we have to God? We don't trust He really will throw open the floodgates of blessing in return.

> "Bring the whole tithe into the storehouse, that there may be food in my house. Test me in this," says the LORD Almighty, "and see if I will not throw open the floodgates of heaven and pour out so much blessing that there will not be room enough to store it" (Malachi 3:10).

Sacrificial giving is one of the few times God asks us to test Him, yet for many years I found myself unwilling to accept the challenge. I was willing to tithe but not willing to go beyond what I felt comfortable giving. Leaving our comfort zone, however, is the very place God calls us to. He wants us to venture into truly abundant giving. He wants us to get out from under our own self-ishness with our possessions and accept His invitation to become radically obedient with what we own. Then, not only will He bless us, but He will lavish blessing upon blessing on us.

I saw this firsthand when I was saving money for a new outfit.

I started this "new outfit fund" because of an embarrassing situation I found myself in during a country club speaking engagement. I was wearing what I thought was a nice outfit, but when I showed up at the event, I quickly realized that not only was my outfit a little out of style, but my white discount store shoes were the only light-colored foot apparel in the entire building. (Not being a queen of fashion, I was unaware of the rule that white shoes have to wait until after Memorial Day in some parts of the country.) Everyone had on dark-colored shoes, so with every step I took, I felt as though my feet were screaming, "White shoes! Everyone look at my shocking white shoes!"

You'll be happy to know that not even white shoes could stop me from sharing about Jesus with this lovely group of women, but you'd better believe I was determined to update and improve my wardrobe.

It took me a while, but I managed to save up one hundred dollars in my "new outfit fund," so I set a date to go shopping with some of my fashion-savvy friends. Just a few days before I was to go shopping, another dear friend phoned to ask me to pray for her family's financial situation. They could not make ends meet and had many bills they were unable to pay. She mentioned they needed one hundred dollars immediately. While she was only asking me to pray for her and nothing more, I knew God was looking for a response from me that would honor Him. I prayed for my friend and then I obeyed God's prompting to give to her the money I'd saved.

The day arrived for my shopping trip, and I must admit that instead of being excited, I felt a pang of dread. I knew that because I had given my money away, I could only look and not purchase anything. I didn't want my fashion friends to think I was wasting their time, so I decided I would put whatever clothes they picked out for me on hold and pray that God would provide the means to return later and purchase them.

While I was moping about and strategizing, God was at work in my friends' hearts. After trying on three beautiful outfits complete with shoes and accessories, I returned to my dressing room to try and decide which outfit to put on hold. While I dressed, my friends took everything to the checkout counter and treated me to a $700 shopping spree!

"'Test me in this,' says the LORD Almighty, 'and see if I will not throw open the floodgates of heaven and pour out so much blessing that there will not be enough room to store it.'" I was shocked and humbled that God had taken the little gift I'd given to my friend and returned it sevenfold through other friends.

The Life That Is Truly Life

The apostle Paul wrote:

> Command those who are rich in this present world not to be arrogant nor to put their hope in wealth, which is so uncertain, but to put their hope in God, who richly provides us with everything for our enjoyment. Command them to do good, to be rich in good deeds, and to be generous and willing to share. In this way they will lay up treasure for themselves as a firm foundation for the coming age, so that they may take hold of the life that is truly life (1 Timothy 6:17-19).

In this country, I think we would agree that most of us are "rich" and this passage applies to us. So what motivates us to venture out into the area of sacrificial giving—an area that for many of us is a real stretch? There are two radical blessings tucked within Paul's words here. The first, which is also referenced in Matthew 6, speaks of laying up treasures in heaven—sending that which we cannot take with us ahead where we can enjoy it and benefit from it in eternity. If you knew you could immediately enjoy a treasure for one day or enjoy it forever if you waited just a short while, which would you choose? In this light, the eternal route makes so much more sense.

The second blessing goes hand in hand with the first. God is aware of our humanness and our desire for instant gratification. He tends to that as well. Not only are we blessed for eternity when we give, but we are blessed for today too: "So that they may take hold of the life that is truly life."

To live the life that is "truly life" is to live abundantly in the here and now. In his book *The Treasure Principle,* Randy Alcorn wrote:

> The act of giving is a vivid reminder that it's all about God, not about us. It's saying I am not the point, *He* is the point. He does not exist for me. I exist for Him. God's money has a higher purpose than my affluence. Giving is a joyful surrender to a greater person and a greater agenda. Giving affirms Christ's lordship. It dethrones me and exalts Him. It breaks the chains of mammon that would enslave me. As long as I still have something, I believe I own it. But when I give it away, I relinquish control, power and prestige. At the moment of release the light turns on. The magic spell is broken. My mind clears. I recognize God as owner, myself as servant, and others as intended beneficiaries of what God has entrusted to me.[1]

If we choose to obey and give of our resources in abundance, a feeling of amazing satisfaction will follow. The radical blessing of being able to take hold of a real life—a fulfilled and satisfied life we can't find any other way—will be ours.

Just Give Me Five Minutes

Dane and Kema Kovach are friends of ours who just a few years ago seemed as though they were on the fast track to the American dream. Dane was an orthodontist with a thriving practice. He was a dedicated family man, leader in our church, and avid outdoorsman. Kema was a terrific mother of four precious adopted children and busy making plans to build their dream home. They had land, architectural drawings, and beautiful decorating plans. Just a few months before they were to break ground, our church started a building campaign that would allow us to move from our temporary high school auditorium home to a real building we could call our own.

During this campaign many amazing stories of sacrifice began to surface within the families of our church. The Kovaches were no exception. God began stirring in Dane's heart and Kema's heart individually. Both were nervous about sharing with the other the absolute radical direction they felt God leading them in. Just a few weeks before the commitment ceremony, where the leaders of the church promised the firstfruits of the building offering, they both sheepishly approached a conversation they had to have. Imagine their shock as they realized God was speaking to both of them about sacrificing the money they'd saved for their dream home.

Joyfully, they placed their dreams in God's hands and invested their finances for eternity.

This act set their hearts on fire for God. After that big decision, every time I saw Dane and Kema the joy of

Yes Factor

Obedience to God sets off a chain reaction of divine change. You'll change. Those around you will change. Even the world can change.

the Lord radiated from them. It wasn't long afterward that Dane went on a mission trip only to return with another shocking revelation from God: Both he and Kema felt they were being called to the mission field.

Just before they left, they proudly stood before our congregation and gave some insights from their amazing adventure with God during the years leading up to their departure for Papua New Guinea.

Dane was quick to give an answer to the questions swirling about them during their time of preparation to leave. "When people ask me why I'm doing all this, selling my thriving practice, taking my family of six on the mission field for four years, giving up what most consider the American dream, I have to point to the overwhelming joy and fulfillment I feel at this point in my life in my relationship with the Lord. I only wish I could place my heart inside the person questioning me and let them experience this joy I feel for just five minutes."

I have a feeling that if each of us could taste that deep joy for those five minutes, our world would be a dramatically different place. We would go out of our way every moment of every day seeking ways to give.

But most of us have grown up with upside-down thinking. We fear giving sacrificially will make our lives empty, when in reality withholding is what leads to emptiness. Stop and think about that for a moment. Even on the simplest level this is true. If you've ever withheld a word of congratulations from a friend because you were jealous of their achievement, you know the emptiness of that stinginess. Giving, releasing, and surrendering to God in this way is what leads to more fulfillment than we ever dreamed possible.

We too can experience this same transformation and wave of

lasting strength that Dane and Kema experienced. We only need to be willing to say yes to God. The extra special part of such a decision is that God will completely customize the life He has for you. Your yes will likely not lead to Papua New Guinea. (It may, but it probably won't.) Your yes may lead you to start a prayer group at school. It may lead you on mission trips and lead you to have a heart for other nations and people, like my daughter Hope is experiencing. Your yes may inspire you to walk in God's strength to try something you've never done, such as write or volunteer or start cooking meals for a local shelter. You can't begin to imagine the amazing things that will unfold. But God does!

Seeing Beyond Our Front Step

I must admit I am sometimes tempted to become consumed with all the ministry opportunities just within the walls of the TerKeurst home. Having five kids is a delightful but daunting task at times. Yet while my family is my primary ministry, it is not my only ministry.

God has placed the desire in my heart to reach out past my family and myself to look for opportunities to live a sacrificial life that touches others for Christ. While God has not called me to the mission field on foreign soil, He has called me to a life of mission work in this place He has me now. Sometimes these "others" I'm called to reach out to are complete strangers whom I touch for a moment and pray God will use me to draw their hearts closer to Him. Other times the opportunities I'm blessed with are with people I know and come in contact with often enough to see God's bigger plan after I play my small role. Such was the case with my dear friend Genia one evening as we gathered with a couple of our close friends for dinner.

Genia and I are part of a small group of very close friends. We call our group "ASAP," which stands for Accountability, Sharing our dreams, Asking the tough questions, and Praying for one another. One night during our meeting, Genia was sharing a tough place she found herself in. As she described her situation, it reminded me of a song on my favorite CD. The Christian artist who sang the song perfectly described what it is like to be caught between life before really living for Christ and life where you sense God leading. This longing to go back and yet the desire to move ahead into a deeper walk with Christ was the place my friend found herself. I knew I had to let Genia hear this song.

After dinner I asked her to walk to my car with me to listen to the CD. I was in the process of telling her how I had this CD on continual play in my car because I loved it so much when God interrupted my thoughts and told me to give it to her.

As the song played, Genia had tears in her eyes and told me it perfectly described how she was feeling. I pushed the eject button, placed the CD in its plastic case, and handed it to her. I told her that God wanted her to have this CD, so now it was hers. Instead of listening to the music as I made my way home that night, I sat in silent prayer for my friend. It was a beautiful ride home.

The next day, Genia called with such excitement in her voice that she could hardly contain herself. She said she had listened to the song over and over. Then she remembered something that brought her to her knees. Three weeks earlier she'd attended a special prayer service where a woman whom Genia did not know came over and prayed with her. The woman told Genia that God loved her, He understood where she was, He promised not to leave her, and that He would give her a song to minister to her. "A song, Lysa, a song!" she exclaimed. "God promised me a song, and He used your hands to deliver it last night."

Tears welled up in my eyes as I realized that what I thought was a simple gift had actually been a well-timed God event for my friend's life. But the blessing didn't end there. Later that same day, the vice president of a large ministry called me on my cell phone. She said God had given her an idea for special retreats to reach women all across the country. She told God that she would write down any names that came to her mind as possible leaders for these retreats. She took out a piece of paper and instantly three names came to mind. She wrote her own name at the top. She then wrote two other names that had really been on her heart: mine and the Christian artist of the CD I had given to Genia.

All I did was give away a CD.

You're Invited…
to Plan a Giving Spree

WHAT:
Set in motion a fabulous spree of generosity that will lead to great joy and a hunger to keep on giving!

WHEN:
Pray about what you want to give and about which person or people will receive your gift. Then decide on the time frame. Don't wait too long to indulge in this amazing experience.

WHERE:
You decide! You might want to go on a giving spree at:

- home—make breakfast for your family for a week or plan a family devotion time

- church—lead a small group and help other girls build a strong spiritual foundation

- school—tutor a classmate or start a teacher appreciation week

- neighborhood—offer free once-a-week babysitting to a family who could use the break

- community—volunteer to help at a nursing home or a local hospital once a month

- a place you've never been—raise money to mail needed school supplies to kids in another country or start raising money to go on a mission trip

These are just a few ideas to spark your creativity.

WHAT TO BRING:
Whatever you decide you want to give. And also bring an attitude of sacrifice, praise, and joy.

Faith in Action, Heart at Rest

Contrary to what the world might tell us, sacrificial giving leads to beautiful opportunities and experiences. The many views we are exposed to say it's best to grab everything you can, when you can, no matter the consequences. That is in opposition to the yes journey, which leads us to amazing chances to give of ourselves and to give without restriction and expectations. This kind of all-out giving leads to the happiness and joy our hearts long for. The apostle John put it this way: "Dear children, let us not love with words or tongue but with actions and in truth. This is how we know that we belong to the truth and how we set our hearts at rest in his presence" (1 John 3:18-19).

Our faith is supposed to be active, three-dimensional, and lived out. And our hearts are to be at rest in God's presence. Being active and resting in God's presence sounds like two different modes of living, doesn't it? But these two are connected, and we can live these out through our extraordinary stories. I'm convinced doing this very thing is a treasure in life very few experience. So how do we find this heart at rest? Through actions and in truth. I have moments where my heart is at rest in His presence, but these moments are broken up by pitfalls and pity parties. Sometimes I just simply want to be selfish, and yet when I choose selfishness I may be happy for the moment, but I'm miserable in the long run.

Yet God, with His incredible patience, doesn't leave me in my misery. I call out to Him in repentance, and, just like a connect-the-dots game, Jesus fills in the gaps between the dots to reveal a beautiful picture of Himself in my life. What if there were less and less space between my dots, revealing an even clearer picture of Christ in my life at all times? If only I could learn to practice the presence of Christ at every moment, in every decision, and with all I come in contact with. Setting my heart at rest in His presence in this way comes with practice and maturity. The more I practice His presence, the more I will experience His presence, and the more mature I will become. And when you and I experience God more fully, our giving and sharing and other sacrificial actions are done with greater ease and from our heart.

Elizabeth George talks about the process of maturity in a beautiful way:

> The Old Testament term for the word gentleness, *anah*, describes a mature, ripened shock of grain with its head bent low and bowed down. Just think for a moment on the beauty of this word picture. As wheat grows, the young sprouts rise above the rest. Their heads shoot up

the highest because no grain has yet formed. In their immaturity, little fruit, if any, has appeared. But, as time passes and maturity sets in, fruit comes forth—so much of it that the burdened stalk bends and its head sinks lower and lower—and the lower the head the greater amount of fruit.[2]

Lord, help me to lower my head past my selfishness and pride, past desiring others to serve me and on to serving others, past wanting more and on to giving more, past me in search of You. Help me to always desire the lowered head, full of Your fruit and consumed with Your presence. Help me to be forever mindful of my ministry at home as well as the ministry opportunities that wait beyond my own mailbox.

God owns it all. We are simply managers of His resources. When we pursue beautiful opportunities of sacrificial living, we freely acknowledge that truth and then reap the blessings. When we come to understand that we're giving up what was never ours to begin with, we're walking in extraordinary faithfulness.

God's Word for You

Read Psalm 81:8-16. Now let's break down some of the verses to unearth the rich treasures contained within.

First, look at verse 9:

> "You shall have no foreign god among you; you shall not worship any god other than me."

Though our hearts are not often tempted to bow down to statues and gods of other religions, we are often tempted to bow down to material things. What tempts you to pull your focus off God?

It's a sign of trouble when we hold on to these things so tightly that the idea of releasing them causes great turmoil in our spirit. Often these things aren't even bad things; they just aren't God's best. As Jim Collins in his business book called *Good to Great* points out, sometimes the enemy to great is often settling for good. Write a description of what many consider to be the "good life."

Now contrast that with what God would define as "the great life."

Read verse 10 from Psalm 81: "I am the LORD your God, who brought you up out of Egypt. Open wide your mouth and I will fill it." There are three key points from this verse.

First, a reminder of the fact that the Lord is our God. Why is it important for us to keep that in our minds at all times?

Second, He is our God, who has been faithful throughout our journey and delivered us. What does this mean to you personally?

Third, if we open ourselves up to Him fully, He will fill us. What does opening ourselves up to Him fully mean?

Verse 16 says:

> "You would be fed with the finest of wheat; with honey from the rock I would satisfy you."

What does temporary satisfaction look like?

What does real satisfaction look like?

Do you believe God is capable of truly satisfying you?

Verses 11 and 12 warn us about being self-focused, close fisted, and stubborn hearted:

> "My people would not listen to me; Israel would not sub-
> mit to me. So I gave them over to their stubborn hearts
> to follow their own devices."

What were the consequences for the Israelites not listening to God, not trusting God, and constantly complaining to God? Find an example in the Old Testament of Israel following their own devices and suffering because of it. If you are having a hard time knowing where to start, look in Numbers 11:1,4; 14:1-4; or 20:2-3.

List their complaint, their sin, and their consequence.

Living Y.E.S. (Your Extraordinary Story)

What are you holding tightly to right now that you feel you are supposed to give to God as a willing offering?

Select a verse from this chapter or from your personal Scripture reading time that encourages you to trust God with this particular area of life. Write the verse in this space and read it or say it from memory each day until you have made your offering.

Describe a time when you received a gift from someone and it felt like a direct gift from God. How did that impact you and your faith?

Plan a "Spree with Me" event. Invite friends near you or those on Facebook or Twitter to join in with ideas to do their own giving spree wherever they live and however they can.

In this chapter we read,

> "Dear children, let us not love with words or tongue but with actions and in truth. This is how we know that we belong to the truth, and how we set our hearts at rest in his presence" (1 John 3:18-19).

How do you plan to apply these verses to your life?

What is the promise in store for you when you apply this truth?

Once you start giving freely and freely giving your life to God, your faith story will be transformed in amazing ways. List ideas for how you can share the love of God with others in practical and extraordinary ways through your talents, blessings, opportunities, and faithfulness.

-
-
-

Yes Prayer

God, I want to be a great giver! And I want to praise You all the while. Show me how the blessings I've already received can now be shared with others. Remind me that when I am worrying about which of my many shirts I want to wear that there is a girl somewhere near me who wishes she had a choice. When I'm complaining about my family being overly protective, show me who in my life needs to know that someone cares about their well-being. And when I receive the blessing of great joy from learning to give freely and abundantly, show me how to share the gift of this excitement and faith with others! These small acts of faithfulness can change the world. Thank You, God! Nobody plans better surprises than You. I can't wait to experience the spiritual blessings of giving. In Jesus' name, amen.

8

The Blessing Found in Yes

The other day I was driving down a busy road when I came upon a traffic light that was both green and red at the same time. Unsure of what to do, I slowed, as did other cars coming from all directions. It was a confusing and dangerous situation. Some people stopped, others ran through the light, and still others pulled off to the side of the road.

I finally made it through the intersection. A little later I thought about the incident. It was as if God were showing me a visual picture of what it's like when a person is indecisive in her obedience to Him. We can't follow God wholeheartedly if part of our heart is being pulled in a different direction. We can't pursue the radically obedient life and still continue to flirt with disobedience in certain areas. We can't be both red and green toward God at the same time. It gets us nowhere. It's confusing. It's dangerous.

This book has been your invitation to become a woman who says yes to God and catch a glimpse of the blessings that are ahead. Now it's time to respond.

Don't be afraid, my friend. I know your mind may be flooded with the same questions that flooded my mind as I was responding to this invitation.

"What if I don't feel able to make such a commitment?"

"What if I say yes and then mess up?"

"What if my inabilities make God look bad?"

"What if I have times when I just don't feel like being obedient?"

Let's go back to my husband's wise advice: Consider the source. Who is asking these questions? That's not your voice sowing seeds of doubt; it's Satan's voice. He wants to keep you in fear and confusion. He wants you to pull off to the side of the intersection and remain ineffective. He wants you to fail to fulfill the purposes God has for you and thwart the positive impact you could make in the lives of so many.

You don't feel able? Good! Christ's power is made perfect in weakness (2 Corinthians 12:9). Ask God for the strength to persevere every day. Ask God for the desire to remain radically obedient and for spiritual eyes to see the radical blessings He will shower upon you.

What if you mess up? Grace! "God opposes the proud but shows favor to the humble. Submit yourselves, then, to God. Resist the devil, and he will flee from you. Come near to God and he will come near to you…humble yourselves before the Lord, and he will lift you up" (James 4:6-8,10). Please don't think I walk this radical obedience journey with perfection, because I don't. Chances are you won't either. But God doesn't expect perfection from us— He expects a person humble enough to admit her weaknesses and committed enough to press through and press on. He will guide us past the doubts and fears and lift us up to fulfill our calling.

What if you wake up in a bad mood and just don't feel like being obedient? Choice! Obey based on your decision to obey, not on your ever-changing feelings. *I don't feel like giving. I don't feel like smiling. I don't feel like listening to God.* But here's what God has to say about that: "It is *God* who works in you to will and to act in order to fulfill his good purpose" (Philippians 2:13, emphasis added). When we ask God to continually give us the desire to remain obedient, He does. He will help us to want to obey Him and will give us His power to do so.

Get Ready!

If your answer is no to radical obedience, then let it be no. I just ask you to do one thing while you sit at the red light. Pray that God will give you the desire to say yes. Let me challenge you for the next 30 days to pray and ask God to reveal Himself to you and fill you with a desire for Him like never before. Remember that lasting obedience must be born out of desire, not duty. Choose to be a woman who says yes to God by starting with this simple prayer. It will cost you only a minute of your time each day, but it will bless you for a lifetime!

If your answer to this invitation is yes, then get ready. You have not only signed up for the most incredible journey you can imagine, but you've also just given God the green light to pour out His radical blessings on your life! What I'm writing about here is just a glimpse of how God will bless you. He's capable of so much more!

Deeper Relationship with God

You will begin to live in expectation of hearing from God every day. You will start to better understand His character and seek to be more like Him. You will discover the depth of love the Father has for you that you never even knew was possible. This will give you a feeling of acceptance and significance you can't get any other way.

Some people spend their whole lives chasing things they think will make them feel accepted and significant, but the truth is this world only has packages full of empty promises to offer. The new house, the fancier car, the latest gadget, the fastest computer, the sleek fashions, and everything else that seems so enticing won't last. They will all wear out, break down, tear up, and become obsolete. Five, ten, twenty years from now, they won't look so appealing and will have to either be updated or replaced. Fifty years from now, most will be taking up space in a junkyard somewhere.

In contrast, every investment we make in our relationship with God will only serve to reap rich dividends for now and eternity. No time spent experiencing God will ever be a waste.

More Adventurous Life

The reality is sometimes life is hard. Yet the Bible says that each day is a gift from God we should rejoice in (Psalm 118:24). Daily adventures with God will add an excitement to your life that will change your whole perspective. No longer is your day just one boring task after another, but rather a string of divine appointments and hidden treasures waiting to be discovered.

Seeing life like this opens up God's floodgates of joy. The mark of a truly godly woman is one who reveals the power of God not so much in her doing as in her being. She has opened God's treasure chest of joy and so filled her heart with gratitude and love that just being around her inspires you. She goes about the simplest of tasks, her everyday duties, and even the rough patches of life with such grace that you find yourself wanting to imitate her. She is full of adventure yet not worn out from the journey.

Depth of Inner Peace

In our world of turmoil and uncertainty, there is nothing more precious than peace. When we say yes to God, we know our life and the lives of those we love rest in the certainty of His never-changing love for us. While we can't control the circumstances we face, we can choose how we react to them. If you've settled in your heart to say yes to God and completely trust Him, then you don't have to worry about the future. You are not in charge of the outcome; you are simply responsible to be obedient. You will be blessed with the peace of knowing that God has a perfect plan and holds everything in His perfect control. What freedom this brings!

Personal Satisfaction

Radically obedient people no longer have to strategize and manipulate things into happening. Instead, they are blessed with opportunities that bring them real satisfaction according to God's perfect design for them. When my husband and I adopted our sons from Liberia, I thought the responsibility of adding more children would mean the end of my ministry, but that has not been the case. God has grown the ministry, sent more people to help run it, and blessed us with the most amazing opportunities to tell our adoption story. We've been allowed to freely talk about listening and obeying God on *Good Morning America, The Oprah Winfrey Show,* and in *O, The Oprah Magazine.* God has taken our obedience and maximized our ministry's impact.

Better Relationships with People

In every relationship with others, you will find things you love and things that get on your nerves. The radically obedient person is blessed with being able to appreciate another's Christlikeness and to give grace to their humanness. Whether a person is a believer or not, he is still made in God's image, and God is crazy in love with him. When you are committed to radical obedience, you see everyone through God's eyes of love.

Meaning and Purpose to Life

Author Bruce Wilkinson wrote:

> Once the Lord has fed His child through intimate devotions, He begins to call him more pointedly to deeper obedience. At this point, the believer desires more of the Lord so much that he is more than willing to do whatever the Lord requires…Obedience for this individual is no longer a burden, undertaken only because the Bible tells him to do something. Rather, obedience becomes a joy because his closest friend and most compassionate Lord beckons him to be like Him.[1]

Our hearts search for deeper meaning in life, and radically obedient people find it in loving the Lord, loving others He brings in our path, and continually seeking to become more like Jesus.

Eternal Perspective

Life is about so much more than just the here and now, and the radically obedient person lives in light of that perspective. Life isn't about being comfortable and taking the easiest route. It's about living to give our lives away and making a real impact in this world. It's not about serving out of religious duty. It's about delighting in our relationship with God so much that we want to serve out of an overflow of love and gratitude. Our time here is but a small dot on an eternal line. What we do now in this brief moment will determine our destiny for eternity. The radically obedient person is blessed with an eternal perspective.

Yes Factor

God leads you out of your comfort zone so you'll depend on Him. He wants you to be comfort-*able*—able to gather His comfort and share it.

An Extraordinary Story Example

I am drawn to the story of one New Testament woman who was radically obedient—Mary, Lazarus's sister. I am moved by her overwhelming love for Jesus. She was a woman who understood the essence of radical obedience. She knew when to listen and when to act. She knew when to simply sit at the Master's feet and when to pour out all she had in lavish love for her Lord (Matthew 26:6-13).

Jesus had just announced He would be crucified. Mary took what was probably her most costly possession, the perfume from her alabaster jar, and poured it out on Him. Normally, one would pour perfume on a dead body, but Mary anointed Jesus while He was still living. I believe it was so Jesus could carry the scent of her love with Him to the cross.

Mary was scolded by some of the disciples for her act of extravagance (naysayers!), but Jesus was quick to jump to her defense. What others saw as waste, He saw as the purest form of walking out the gospel message. She was willing to love Him without reservation, without concern for what others might think or even concern for herself. Mary showed an unabashed love through this act, and, make no mistake, Jesus was quick to lavish His love right back on her. "I tell you the truth," He said, "wherever the gospel is preached throughout the world, what she has done will also be told, in memory of her" (Matthew 26:13).

Isn't it amazing that such a small act of obedience could have such far-reaching effects? That can happen in our lives as well. It's easy to see that Mary was radically obedient and radically blessed… and you can be too.

You're Invited...
to Accept God's Will for You

WHAT:

Together we've explored how God has used the yeses of myself, Hope, and many others. And you've had a chance to say yes to God in different ways as well.

WHEN:

Now and forever. God's will unfolds in His unique timing for each of us. Keep your heart and hands open to what God will ask you to receive.

WHERE:

Right where you are. That's the beauty of the yes journey. God may take you out of your comfort zone to places you've never even dreamed of going, but He will meet you where you're at so you don't have to take steps alone. You will move forward together.

WHAT TO BRING:

Keep your journal with you and use it to write letters to God and to explore how He speaks to you through His Word.

Are there any items you want to add as you keep growing as a young woman who says yes to God? (Maybe you've added some prayerful friends or mentors.) Also, keep this book with your Bible study and Living Y.E.S. comments near you so you can refer back to these lessons and to see how you've grown in a few months, a year, and beyond.

How It Ends

Well, this whole adventure began with God telling me to give away my Bible, so is it any surprise that it ends the same way? I recently flew to the Washington, DC, area for a speaking engagement. The man next to me on the plane was busy working on his computer and did not appear to be in the mood to be interrupted. My heart kept feeling drawn to share the gospel with him, but it didn't seem appropriate to force a conversation. So I prayed.

I prayed that God would prompt *him* to start talking to me. And talk he did. It wasn't long before he put his computer away and started asking me all kinds of questions about my career. Because I write and speak about Jesus, this was a perfect opportunity to tell him all about my Boss! When we started talking about God, he said he'd been studying the Koran and several other religious writings, but not the Bible. However, he'd called the friend he was traveling to see and asked if they could buy a Bible that weekend to complete his collection.

I almost fell out of my seat. Of all the planes traveling to Washington that day and of all the people who were seated together, God arranged for a man who needed a Bible to sit beside a woman who loves to give Bibles away! I shared with my new friend my passion for giving away Bibles, and I promised I would send him one the next week. He sat stunned. When he finally spoke again, he told me he knew this was more than sheer coincidence. He knew God was reaching out to him.

We don't have to seek to create opportunities to say yes to God. He has already gone before us and established them. We simply have to respond.

I pray the end of this book is not the conclusion of your journey. I sincerely hope this is only the starting place, the point of inspiration and expression for you to live a radically obedient, radically blessed life.

God's Word for You

For this concluding Bible study, we are going to do something a little different. God's Word has much to say on the topic of saying yes to Him and the amazing blessings that follow. Pick ten of these key verses, look them up for yourself, and discover what God wants you to know about His calling on your life. I've summarized the verses, but it will be so much more powerful to dig into God's Word and record the powerful promises yourself.

Deuteronomy 28:1-14	Obedience opens God's storehouse of blessings.
2 Chronicles 16:9	God will strengthen the heart of the obedient person.
Esther 4:14	God has called you to obedience for such a time as this.
Psalm 15	Obedient people dwell in the presence and peace of God.
Psalm 24	Obedience in what you say, what you do, and what you think leads to holiness and blessings from God.
Isaiah 55:1-3	Obedience brings your soul satisfaction, delight, and new life.
Hosea 10:12	Obedience reaps the fruit of unfailing love and brings showers of righteousness.

Malachi 3:8-10	Being obedient givers will open God's storehouse of blessing.
Malachi 3:16-17	Radically obedient people are treasures to God.
Matthew 26:12-13	Even small acts of obedience have widespread effects.
Romans 1:5	Obedience comes from faith.
Romans 6:15-16	Obedience leads to righteousness.
Romans 8:5-6	Those walking in obedience have their minds set on God's desires.
2 Corinthians 9:6	The extent that we sow in obedience will determine the extent we will reap in blessings.
2 Corinthians 9:13	Men will praise God for the obedience that accompanies our faith.
Ephesians 4:24	We were created to be like God. We walk this out in obedience leading to holiness.
Philippians 2:13	It is God working in us that prompts us to be obedient and fulfill His good purpose.
Philippians 4:9	What you have learned, heard, or seen from God, walk it out in obedience and you will be blessed with peace.
2 Timothy 2:20-21	God is able to use the obedient person for His noblest purposes.

Hebrews 11   A list of radically obedient, radically blessed people.

1 Peter 1:13-14   Prepare your mind for obedience, which leads to holiness.

1 Peter 2:21-22   Those who walk in obedience walk in Jesus' footsteps.

1 John 2:3-6   Obedience makes God's love complete in us and enables us to walk as Jesus did.

Living Y.E.S. (Your Extraordinary Story)

If you're anything like me, these chapters, stories, verses, and glimpses of the power of yes get me to thinking and then to asking questions.

- What do you want from me, God?

- What are you asking me to stop holding on to?

- What is my big assignment from You?

Don't ever be afraid to bring anything before the Lord. When we seek His leading and His help, we are growing into young women who say yes to God daily. What other questions do you have for Him right now?

-

-

-

Let's go through your invitations to say yes to God during our time together. Take a moment to determine if you have RSVP'd to each of these yet. Initial those you have said yes to.

Invitation	**RSVP**
You're Invited…to Attend God's Surprise Party for You	
You're Invited…to Begin the Yes Adventure	
You're Invited…to Experience the Sweet Secret Place	
You're Invited…to Trust God Completely	
You're Invited…to Focus on God	
You're Invited…to Trade Duty for Delight!	
You're Invited…to Plan a Giving Spree	
You're Invited…to Accept God's Will for You	

Which of these has been the hardest to say yes to (maybe you still haven't)? Why?

What else have you said yes to during these past weeks? Describe what it feels like to be on this yes journey.

Yes Prayer

This is the prayer that keeps on going. Every minute of every day you are presented with an opportunity to say yes to God's best, His hope for you, and His calling on your life. Write a prayer here that communicates your yes to each of the special invitations. And where you have not yet said yes, ask God for help to do so. You can bring anything to Him. Bring your "no" or your "I don't know" as an offering and ask for strength and courage to transform your no into a yes that lasts a lifetime. Lift up this prayer starter and then keep talking to God as your extraordinary story continues to unfold.

> *God, You are amazing. Your grace and hope changes lives, including mine. I'm so grateful I'm getting to know You better. I feel I can stand strong in my faith even when I have bad days or days of questions. You invite me to embrace the extraordinary no matter what. Today, as I say yes to Your will, I lift up these areas of need, hope, and uncertainty in my life...*

> *Thank You, Lord, for hearing every word I speak, think, whisper, or cry out to You in prayer. You love me and I love You. This is the most important truth in my extraordinary story. In Jesus' name, amen.*

YES IN ACTION: LOOKING FORWARD
A Note from Hope's Yes Journey

"What do you want to be when you grow up?"

Believe me, this is a question you'll hear often as you make your way through high school. I have friends who let that question take over their thoughts, decisions, and worries, but I want to share with you a different way to look toward the future.

Try asking "*Who* do you want to be?"

That's the question I focus on because it challenges me to find my identity and path in God and not through circumstances. Maybe another way to say that is: *Whose* do you want to be?

I want to be God's daughter now and in the future.

At any given moment, if I'm striving to seek God's will and trust His leading, I am doing the right thing. Someone recently asked me how I made the decision to do the first mission trip. When I look at that time in my life, I clearly see God's leading and intervention. The opportunity presented itself through a school requirement. I'm a planner, and I always think through my next steps, but in this case, I just went for it. I had no idea what I was heading into, but God gave me a great peace and the strength to say yes.

This ended up being a life-changing, faith-building, passion-forming event. I would've missed this vital part of my story if I had given over to fears sparked by the "what" questions. *What will happen when I'm there? What will it be like to not have the comforts of home? What if I'm not good at this?*

We can ask these questions until we make ourselves sick with worry, or we can embrace the yes life and the extraordinary story

God is calling us to experience. As for me, I plan to keep asking who I want to be and whose I want to be. When I look beyond the world's expectations and toward God's best for me personally, the future is bright, exciting, purposeful, and incredibly inviting.

Will you join me in the yes adventure?

Let's look forward together...fearless and faithful.

Hope

My Yes Journey Notes

Notes

Chapter 2—Is That You, God?

1. *Life Application Study Bible (NIV)* (Wheaton, IL: Tyndale House Publishers, 1988), 2125.
2. Rick Warren, *The Purpose Driven Life* (Grand Rapids, MI: Zondervan Publishing House, 2002), 233.

Chapter 3—God Wants Your Whole Heart

1. *Life Application Study Bible (NIV)* (Wheaton, IL: Tyndale House Publishers, 1988), 1632.

Chapter 4—Trading Ordinary for Extraordinary

1. *Life Application Study Bible (NIV)* (Wheaton, IL: Tyndale House Publishers, 1998), 2277.
2. A.J. Russell, ed., *God Calling* (Uhrichsville, OH: Barbour Books, 1989), May 19.

Chapter 5—What Keeps Us from Saying Yes

1. Rick Warren, *The Purpose Driven Life* (Grand Rapids, MI: Zondervan Publishing House, 2002), 254.
2. Beth Moore, *Living Free* (Nashville, TN: LifeWay Press, 2001), 82.
3. Ibid., 77.

Chapter 6—Yes Is About Delight

1. Brent Curtis and John Eldredge, *The Sacred Romance* (Nashville, TN: Thomas Nelson, 1997), 137-38.

Chapter 7—Giving Up What Was Never Ours

1. Randy Alcorn, *The Treasure Principle* (Sisters, OR: Multnomah Publishers, 2001), 57.
2. Elizabeth George, *A Woman's Walk with God* (Eugene, OR: Harvest House Publishers, 2000), 172.

Chapter 8—The Blessing Found in Yes

1. Bruce Wilkinson, *Set Apart* (Sisters, OR: Multnomah Publishers, 1998), 175.

About Lysa

Lysa TerKeurst is a wife, mother of five, and the president of Proverbs 31 Ministries. She is the *New York Times* bestselling author of *Unglued* and *Made to Crave,* which remained on the bestsellers list for more than 40 weeks combined. Lysa was recently awarded the Champions of Faith Author Award and has been published in multiple publications such as Focus on the Family and CNN online. Additionally, she has appeared on the *Today Show* as one of the leading voices in the Christian community.

Each year Lysa is a featured keynote presenter at more than 40 events across North America, including the Women of Faith Conferences and the Catalyst Leadership Conference. In addition, she hosts the annual She Speaks Conference, which has helped thousands of women gain the tools to pursue a calling in speaking and writing.

For additional information about Lysa, please visit
www.LysaTerKeurst.com

To find out more on booking Lysa for an event, please e-mail
info@LysaTerKeurst.com

About Proverbs 31 Ministries

Lysa TerKeurst is the president of Proverbs 31 Ministries, located in Charlotte, North Carolina.

If you were inspired by *What Happens When Young Women Say Yes to God* and desire to deepen your own personal relationship with Jesus Christ, we have just what you're looking for.

Proverbs 31 Ministries exists to be a trusted friend who will take you by the hand and walk by your side, leading you one step closer to the heart of God through…

free First 5 app
free online daily devotions
online Bible studies
writer and speaker training
daily radio programs
books and resources

For more information about Proverbs 31 Ministries,
visit www.Proverbs31.org.

To inquire about having Lysa speak at your event,
visit www.LysaTerKeurst.com and click on "speaking."

Other Books by Lysa TerKeurst

Finding I Am

Uninvited

The Best Yes

Becoming More Than a Good Bible Study Girl

Unglued

Made to Crave

What Happens When Women Walk in Faith

To learn more about other books by Lysa TerKeurst

or to read sample chapters, visit our website;

www.harvesthousepublishers.com

HARVEST HOUSE PUBLISHERS
EUGENE, OREGON